MATT&SHARI
great weekend projects™

By Shari Hiller and Matt Fox

DRG
Dynamic Resource Group
PUBLISHING

Matt & Shari:
Great Weekend Projects™

By Shari Hiller and Matt Fox

Copyright © 2006 Annie's Attic, DRG Texas LP, Berne, Indiana 46711

Editors Vicki Blizzard, Jeanne Stauffer
Art Director Brad Snow
Publishing Services Manager Brenda Gallmeyer

Associate Editors Sue Reeves, Dianne Schmidt
Assistant Art Director Nick Pierce
Copy Supervisor Michelle Beck
Copy Editor Mary O'Donnell

Graphic Arts Supervisor Ronda Bechinski
Graphic Artists Erin Augsburger, Jessi Butler
Production Assistants Cheryl Kempf, Marj Morgan, Judy Neuenschwander

Photographers Gary Yasaki/yasakiphotographic.com; Matt Owen
Contributing Photographer Scott Campbell

Chief Executive Officer John Robinson
Publishing Director David McKee
Project Coordinator Linda May
Sales Director John Boggs

Printed in China.
First Printing 2006
Library of Congress Number 2005933216
Hardcover ISBN-10: 1-59635-071-7 ISBN-13: 978-1-59635-071-7
Softcover ISBN 1-59635-108-X ISBN-13: 978-1-59635-108-0

Every effort has been made to ensure the accuracy and completeness of the instructions and information in this book. However, we cannot be responsible for human error or for variations in individual work.

Thanks to those who have provided materials for projects and photographs in this book: Blue Mountain Wallcoverings, Habegger Ace Lumber, Hunter Douglas Window Fashions, Jo-Ann Etc. and Sherwin-Williams.

Permission granted for use of chromes from Dengerd & Pak Photo Productions, Inc.
  Apple Tree Mural, 41
  Cafe Awning, 145
  Hot Air Balloon Mural, 44
  Monogram Book Stand, 180
  Palm Tree Mural, 45
  Picket-Fence Headboard, 6, 38, 40
  Reversible Valance, 142, 144
  Whimsical Birdhouse Cabinet, 20, 26
  Whimsical Lighthouse Cabinet, 21, 26
  Whimsical Cloud Cornice Board, 32

In fond memory of John Robinson, CEO of Dynamic Resource Group, a most courteous, gracious man with a strong sense of honor... a true gentleman. We miss you.

Acknowledgments and thanks from Matt & Shari: We would like to thank all of the fans who have supported us through 11 years of room-by-room decorating. Thanks to the thousands who have come out to see us in our live appearances, and those that visit mattandshari.com on a regular basis. Your stories, your project photos, your questions and comments bring us pure joy. We only hope we can do the same for you.

A heartfelt thank you goes out to my mom, **Pat,** for inspiring me at a young age to try to fix things. It taught me to never give up and that you can fix just about anything with a butter knife!

Special thanks to my family **Bruce and Brittany,** for their interest and support, and especially to my son **Cameron** for demanding that his bubble bedroom be part of the book. "Cam, it's a great project that neither one of us has the patience to do!"

HOME & GARDEN TELEVISION

1 2 3 4 5 6 7 8 9 10

Welcome!

What better way to get started on your next weekend project than with us right by your side? We wish we could do that, but instead we're bringing you the next best thing. The pages that follow will take you step by step through some of our favorite weekend projects.

Welcome! In our first book, *Matt & Shari Real Decorating for Real People*, we introduced you to "Getting Started." This "getting started" time is all the time you spend designing your new room with both function and mood in mind. Once the planning is complete, it's time to do all the projects that make your house a home, and that's where this book comes in.

We begin with Signature Projects, those you've come to love and expect from us. These are projects that we are proud of and have particularly enjoyed creating over the years. Background Projects, as you've come to know, means ceiling and wall treatments. A weekend project book wouldn't be complete without Shop Projects and Sewing Projects! Last, there is a collection of Accessory Projects in case you want to try something smaller to get your feet wet in this wonderful world of decorating.

Our best advice as you begin a project is to read over the instructions carefully and imagine how the pieces go together. Take your time, find a friend to work with you (we always have more fun when we are working together) and enjoy the project each step of the way. Pizza breaks and an unending supply of candy kisses are also a must. Enjoy!

Shari   *Matt*

Contents

SIGNATURE PROJECTS

When you happen upon something you consistently do very well, it becomes your signature. The projects on the next few pages present some of our signature techniques. They are so versatile, we've used them in just about every room in a home … so we've had a lot of practice!

Angles–A New Slant To Floor Plans

An angled arrangement in a room completely changes the way the room feels without adding or subtracting any furniture or accessories. It's one of those decorating tools that doesn't cost a dime—but will give your room a great designer slant!

Get started!

Look at the room to determine the traffic pattern. Do you enter your living room through a foyer and travel through to the dining room? That's a very common scenario. Consider that as the dividing line through the room. More often than not, after you've drawn that imaginary line, one side of the room will end up larger than other. The larger side should be the conversation area, and the smaller side can serve in a variety of ways.

Generally, a larger piece of furniture, such as the sofa, works well placed in a corner of the larger part of the room. Keeping the imaginary line in mind, use it as a guide and place the sofa parallel to that line. Add a pair of chairs at one end of the sofa, or split them up and place one at either end.

The area behind the sofa can be a challenge to fill. A few silk ficus or palm trees can be wonderful if they are of varying heights and lighted from the floor. Floor lighting through the leaves will create fabulous shadows on the wall and ceiling, and give the room instant atmosphere. During the holidays, place a string of tiny white lights among the branches for holiday joy. These lights look nice in the branches all year long and add mood lighting to the room.

Another option for the space behind the sofa is a tall sofa table. A table is practical because it can hold a lamp at one or both ends to bring more warmth to the room. If the lamp is short or too low behind the sofa, prop the lamp on a stack of books until it is the height you need. Arrange a variety of decorative items and small plants in addition to the lamp for extra interest. Or try creating a large painted panel to lean against the wall (see page 72).

An area rug also works well in the larger conversation area of the

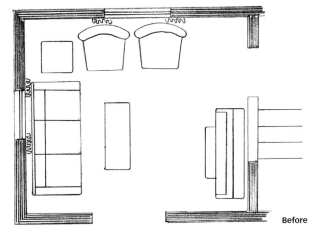

Before

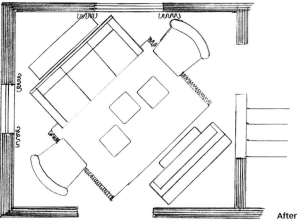

After

From Shari

Everyone I work with, from Matt to the design team to the production crew, says that it's "Shari's patented angle" that makes the room. Well, we all know that I haven't patented the angle, but I'll claim it any day!

room. Placed parallel to the sofa, the rug further reinforces the angle and directs traffic through the room. Make sure you have enough table space for lamps and accessories. As for the smaller side of the room, consider placing a large piece there to serve as a focal point. Matt and I worked on a living room that contained an antique upright piano. Placed at an angle on the smaller side of the room, it became a wonderful focal point. We used the top of it as a display space for a few additional antique pieces, and it was a lovely sight from the conversation area as well as from the front door. Other options for the small side of the room include a desk or home office. Keep it open and functioning during the week, and close it up as a nice accent in the room when entertaining. A group of bookcases lined up in a corner could become

the library you've always wanted. Add a sofa table or small library table on an angle in front of the shelves and you have a great place to do research or study. This smaller side of the room is also perfect for an armoire with a television inside, or even a stereo system to provide background music.

An angled arrangement can spice up a bedroom, a dining room or even a deck or patio. Aside from the impact of changing the wall color with paint, rearranging the furniture can be one of the simplest and most cost-effective ways to make over a room! ■

Shelves—Beautiful & Functional

Whether you are in a bind for space or just need an area to display a favorite collection, shelves can be the answer to storage problems. Custom-built shelves can be easy to make and are a great solution for hard-to-decorate areas such as hallways, stairways and nooks.

Shelves can be the perfect answer to all sorts of decorating questions, such as:

• Instead of crown molding, which can be difficult to install, what other options are available for adding pizzazz to my upper walls?

• My upstairs hallway has no room for hall tables or settees. What can I do to add decorating interest?

• What can I use instead of my tabletops to display my various collections of photos and small art pieces?

The answer to all of these questions is to add shelves! In fact, shelving can solve stairway issues, narrow alcove dilemmas and high-ceiling problems—and they can even be the foundation for an interactive display of family memories.

As an example, a home that we recently decorated contained a back hallway that was used primarily by family members. This hallway included a garage entry, coat closets, a bathroom entrance and the doorway to a small office. This area was the perfect place for the family to display mementos from vacations and other family memorabilia that might have been too busy or distracting in other areas of the home. By installing eight to 12 shelves of varying lengths, we created an interesting arrangement of very personal

objects, including framed art, family photos, flowers, greenery and candles.

A collection such as this can easily look cluttered, but there are ways to prevent that. Generally, an overall theme can tie together dissimilar items. For instance, a family trip to Paris yielded several photos of the Eiffel Tower, a painting of an alleyway in Paris and a tiny metal Eiffel Tower sculpture. Placing all of these items on one shelf created a theme and kept the collection neat, while the variety of sizes and shapes added interest.

To tie together an entire wall of shelves, choose one unifying factor—color, size, shape, material or theme. A collection of framed items looks best if the frames are in the same or a similar finish. Using like colors in artwork or accessories helps blend a variety of items together. If you add greenery to the shelves, try using

all the same type to continue a cohesive statement.

Consider all of the options for arranging family treasures. Framed pieces can be hung on the wall

above a shelf or placed on the shelf and leaned against the wall. Try hanging an item from a higher shelf for added interest.

Shelves are one of the best solutions for dressing up hard-to-decorate areas, such as hallways and stairways. If the stairs are wide enough, narrow shelves can make the trips up and down quite delightful. These shelves are great for displaying family photos and memorabilia, but also consider using them to display a fabulous collection of seashells, vases or antique dolls.

No matter how you look at them, shelves are both functional and decorative, they are great problem solvers and they are easy to build and install.

The handy shelves above are made with purchased wooden stair treads and heavy-duty L-brackets that come with a snap-on plastic cover to give them decorative flair.

Simply sand the treads, stain and coat with a polyurethane finish, or paint them, then install them on the L-brackets for book-ready shelving with just a few hours of work. ■

Scalloped Accessory Shelf

More than just storage, this shelf has style! The scalloped edge adds feminine flair and makes it appealing to women of all ages.

SHOPPING LIST

18 feet of 1x4 poplar lumber (three 6-foot lengths)

Finish nails

1½-inch drywall screws

Molly bolts or self-anchoring screws

Spackling compound

Desired paint or stain

Primer appropriate for desired paint or stain

Wooden buttons (optional)

MATERIALS ON HAND

Tape measure

Jigsaw with scroll blade

Hammer

150- and 220-grit sandpaper

Tack cloth

Wood glue

Card stock or poster board

Pencil

Scissors

Cordless drill

Paintbrushes

Steps

1 Cut two 1x4 boards to desired length. One board will be the back plate and the other will be the shelf top.

2 Drill several pilot holes and countersink holes along the length of the shelf top. Run a bead of wood glue along the top of the back plate, then secure the two together using drywall screws.

3 Cut remaining piece of poplar 3 inches wide and the length of your shelf. Cut card stock or poster board 3 inches wide. Draw a template for the scallop pattern on one edge of card stock. This can be a series of soft curves, waves or zigzags. **Note:** Draw at least 3 scallops (waves or zigzags) on the template. Place template at the middle of board, keeping straight edges even. Trace the curved edge of the template onto the wood, then move template down the board toward each end, tracing a series of curves. Repeat until the entire board is covered with the edge design.

4 Using the jigsaw with a scroll blade, cut out the design, moving the blade slowly along the traced lines.

5 After cutting, sand the edges using 150-grit sandpaper; repeat sanding with 220-grit sandpaper for a smooth edge.

6 Attach scalloped board to shelf top with a bead of glue, securing with finish nails. Fill all nail holes with spackling compound; sand smooth.

7 Prime and paint the shelf in desired color/finish.

8 To hang the shelf, drill three pilot holes evenly spaced across the length of the back plate. Position the shelf on the wall and secure with molly bolts. Fill the holes with spackling compound and touch up paint with a small foam brush or use wooden buttons painted to match to fill the holes. ■

TIPS

A scroll blade is designed to make intricate cuts, such as the scalloped edge on this shelf. Just remember, the tighter the curve, the slower you should cut. Don't push the blades—they are very thin, so let the saw do the work.

To coordinate a shelf with the room, paint it the same color as the wall or room trim. For contrast, choose a bright color and have some fun with it!

To create a shelf for hanging coats or decorative items, consider attaching peg hooks to the front of the shelf before painting.

From Shari

Always wear safety glasses when cutting wood to protect your eyes against damage from flying bits of sawdust. Did you know you can even purchase prescription safety glasses? Matt has a pair (just don't tell him I told you).

Whimsical Cabinets

It all starts with an inspiration piece—a miniature version of the cabinet you hope to create. We started with an 8-inch painted birdhouse and a 16-inch-tall, lighthouse-shaped wall cabinet, both of which provided great ideas for design, colors, scale and general construction. Hold fast to your dream—this project can be quite an adventure.

Materials for every cabinet will be somewhat different, depending on the project you are trying to create. Read through the materials list and instructions before purchasing materials.

Before you begin: Determine scale. Measure the inspiration piece. If it is 7 inches tall, for example, you may be able to use a 1 inch to 1 foot scale, which will make a 7-foot-tall cabinet. For the 16-inch-tall lighthouse inspiration piece, a scale of 2 inches to 1 foot will make a finished piece about 8 feet tall. If you're using this cabinet for a television, be sure it is wide enough to accommodate both the television and the arms needed to put it in place on the shelf.

Decide on basic materials, such as what thickness of wood will be appropriate for each of the cabinet pieces. We used ½-inch-thick plywood for the sides, ¾-inch for the front doors and ¼-inch for the back for the barn cabinet to help keep down the weight. Another important

consideration—how will you move this large cabinet from the shop to the living room or bedroom? Some construction may have to be done in the room where this piece will be used. Do you want to be able to move the cabinet? Consider adding wheels to the base.

Decide on details. Dissect the inspiration piece (mentally or physically) one piece at a time. Think about what materials can be used for each detail. For instance, our inspiration birdhouse had feet made from wooden beads. While at a lumberyard, we discovered wooden ball finials meant to be used on top of an exterior railing. They were perfect for the feet of our cabinet.

Whimsical Barn Cabinet

Base

1 Cut one 29½ x 44-inch piece from ¾-inch plywood for top of base (A).

2 Cut two 3½ x 44-inch pieces from 1x4 for front and back (B) of base.

3 Cut two 3½ x 28-inch pieces from 1x4 for sides (C) of base.

4 Butt side pieces into front piece and secure with nails and wood glue. Attach back piece the same way.

5 Attach top of base (A) to frame with nails around the perimeter.

6 Attach 5½-inch-tall decorative porch finials to inside corners of frame with screws through top of base.

Shaping the front

1 Cut a 35½ x 72-inch piece from ¾-inch plywood for front (D1). To create the peak, mark the center point at the top edge (17¾ inches from either side). Measure 40 inches up from the bottom on both sides and mark. Using a straightedge and a pencil, draw two lines connecting the top center point with the two side points. Cut the peak.

Draw the doors

1 Measure up 3½ and 35½ inches from the bottom and draw lines across the width at those points. Measure 2¾ inches from each side and draw two vertical lines from the bottom line to the top line. Drill a small starter hole for the jigsaw blade. Cut out and reserve the 30 x 32-inch piece for the doors (E). *Note: Make sure that the cut is precise down the lines since these pieces will be the final doors.*

Framing the front

1 From 1x2, cut a 35½-inch length (F), two 38½-inch lengths (G) and two 29-inch lengths (H). Attach the 35½-inch length (F) to the back side of the front piece with bottom edges flush. Using wood glue and 1¾-inch drywall screws, attach the 38½-inch lengths (G) to the back side of the front piece with side edges flush. Attach the 29-inch lengths (H) to the back side of the front piece with roof edges flush, mitering at angles as necessary. *Note: Save three offcuts from this step for use as shelf supports in a later step.*

Framing the door opening

1 From 1x2, cut two 30-inch length (I) and two 33½-inch lengths (J). Attach with finish nails to back side of front piece around top and sides of door frame.

Doors

1 The doors are made from the 30 x 32-inch piece of ¾-inch plywood that was cut from the front piece. Cut this piece into two 15 x 32-inch pieces (E).

2 Attach doors to door frame with hinges.

Back

1 For back (D2), repeat step 1 of Shaping the Front, using ¼-inch plywood. Use 1-inch drywall screws for the back.

2 Using a spade bit, drill a 1½-inch hole near the bottom so all wiring can be neatly run through the back.

Sides

1 Cut two 24 x 40-inch pieces of ½-inch plywood for sides (K).

2 Determine height of inside shelf (O); by measuring the

height of your television. Attach offcuts from Framing the front step 1 to insides of back and sides with screws through 1x2s into sides for shelf supports.

Roof

1 Cut two 29½ x 45-inch pieces of ¼-inch plywood for roof panels (L).

2 From 1x2, cut two 29½-inch lengths (M) and four 43½-inch lengths (N).

3 Attach lengths of 1x2 to the bottom and both sides of both panels with edges flush. Use nails and wood glue, nailing through the panels into the 1x2.

Inside shelf

1 Cut one 34 x 22½-inch piece of ¾-inch plywood for inside shelf (O).

Assemble

1 Attach sides by nailing through side pieces into the 1x2s on front and back pieces. Keep bottoms of all pieces flush.

2 From 1x4, cut two 24-inch lengths (P) and two 37½-inch lengths (Q) for bottom trim around the cabinet. Attach 24-inch lengths to sides and 37½-inch lengths to front and back, using finish nails.

3 Place shelf inside the structure on the 1x2 shelf supports.

4 Attach roof by screwing through the 1x2s on the front and back pieces into the roof panels, mitering at peak as necessary.

Chimney

1 Cut one 8¼ x 6¼-inch piece from ¼-inch plywood for short side of chimney (R).

2 Cut three 8¼ x 21½-inch pieces from ¼-inch plywood for front, back and long side (S) of chimney.

3 Cut one 11 x 11-inch piece of ½-inch plywood for chimney cap (T).

4 For front of chimney, measure 6¼ inches down from top of 8¼ x 21½-inch piece of plywood (S) and make a mark. Using a straightedge and a pencil, draw a line to connect this mark with the bottom corner on the opposite side. Cut this angle. Repeat for the back of the chimney.

5 Butt the short chimney side piece (R) into the short side of the front piece with top edges flush and secure with nails and wood screws.

6 Butt the long chimney side piece into the long side of the front piece with top edges flush and secure with nails and wood screws.

7 Using nails and glue, attach back of chimney to sides with top edges flush.

8 Center top cap (T) on chimney and secure with nails and glue through top into chimney.

9 Attach chimney to roof using glue and 1¼-inch drywall screws through roof into chimney.

Finishing

1 Fill all nail holes; let dry. Sand surfaces smooth. Prime and paint as desired. Have fun with your paint finishes, the cabinet can be changed seasonally. Check out our finishing ideas at the end to see how we did it. ■

From Matt

Be safe! Power tools can make a project so much easier— but always remember they can be dangerous if not used properly. Always read the instruction book included with the tools and practice safety at all times. After all, we have many more projects to build!

As for plans, we didn't draw actual pattern pieces to size, but we did create many sketches with the desired dimensions. For the boat cabinet, I even created a small scale model out of a file folder to determine the exact shape of the side pieces.

In some cabinet designs, we weren't certain if everything was going to fit together (you should see our scrap pile). So there was a lot of trial and error, lots of error. All of our cabinets of this type are "design as you build" projects, which can be an adventure!

Finishing ideas

A Whimsical Cabinet comes to life with paint! All of the cabinets we have made in the past have come to life as soon as the paint was applied. Since none of the cabinets were going to be exposed to the elements, we didn't have to prime and got straight to the decorative painting.

Both the birdhouse cabinet and the lighthouse cabinet had miniature inspiration pieces for us to use as guides for the painted design. With the row boat and barn design, we used photographs and children's books for ideas when it came to texture and color.

We bought quarts of latex wall paint for the large areas of color, and for details used acrylic craft paints. Roller and roller covers work well for the base coats, and then we used our 2½- to 3-inch latex brushes to paint areas like the contrasting stripe on the lighthouse, or the picket fence on the birdhouse. We also had 1-inch foam brushes on hand for tighter places, and most of the outlining was done with either a foam brush or artist brushes.

The barn cabinet has the most depth to it because we added

| WHIMSICAL BARN CABINET |
| (Actual Sizes) |

P.	T	W	L	#
A	¾"	29½"	44"	1
B	¾"	3½"	44"	2
C	¾"	3½"	28"	2
D1	¾"	35½"	72"	1
D2	¼"	35½"	72"	1
E	¾"	15"	32"	2
F	¾"	1½"	35½"	2
G	¾"	1½"	38½"	4
H	¾"	1½"	29"	4
I	¾"	1½"	30"	2
J	¾"	1½"	33½"	2
K	½"	24"	40"	2
L	¼"	29½"	45"	2
M	½"	1½"	29½"	2
N	¾"	1½"	43½"	4
O	¾"	34"	22½"	1
P	¾"	3½"	24"	2
Q	¾"	3½"	37½"	2
R	¼"	8¼"	6¼"	1
S	¼"	8¼"	21¼"	3
T	¼"	11"	11"	1

more layers and detailing to different areas of the barn. For instance, the roof shingles were made by first painting the entire roof light green, then drawing on the shingle design with a pencil. The dark green was added using a 2½-inch latex brush, and the bristles started at the top (sometimes even extending past the top) of a shingle and brushed down in a feathering fashion to cover about one half of the shingle. This creates a shadow. The next step was to use a black paint pen and really outline the shingles, adding the cracks and

jagged edges. A brown glaze was used over the top, mainly following the black lines of the shingles, but here and there, an aged effect was created as the glaze was brushed over the dark green paint.

A similar process was used on the red barn siding. Black paint pens created the boards and the brown glaze added depth.

The inside of the doors uses a dry-brush technique to add interest. The doors were first painted in the green, and then a blue with a similar value and saturation was

dry-brushed over the top. Dry brushing uses a brush that has been dipped in paint and then dabbed off, leaving the brush somewhat dry, so only a small amount of paint is transferred to the surface.

We practiced our ideas on scraps of cardboard before going to the project, and referred to our faux-painting books to give us even more inspiration!

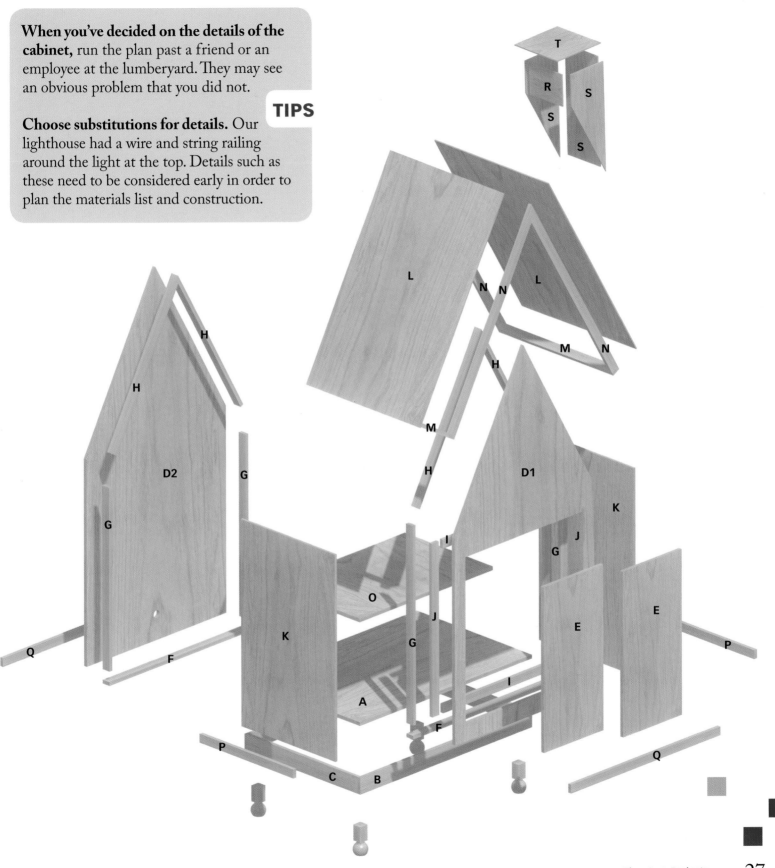

Fabric-Covered Cornice Board

Finish off the top of a window and hide unsightly hardware—a cornice board does both with style! Easy to make, a cornice board can be covered with batting and fabric to add formal elegance to any room.

SHOPPING LIST

Fabric

Quilt batting

¼-inch plywood

**1x4 pine (use 1x6 or wider
if cornice board will be
placed over draperies)**

Finish nails

3-inch L-brackets

1¼-inch drywall screws

MATERIALS ON HAND

Tape measure

Circular saw

**Staple gun with ¼-inch
staples**

**Cordless drill with
Phillips bits**

Project notes

Materials listed will vary
depending on size and shape
of window treatment.

The cornice board is built in two
steps: the frame and the facing.
After the facing is attached to
the frame, the batting and fabric
are attached.

Use high- or low-loft quilt batting
as desired. High-loft will result in
a more padded look; low-loft in a
less padded look. Just be sure to
leave at least 2 inches between
the finished cornice board and
any window treatment it may
be covering.

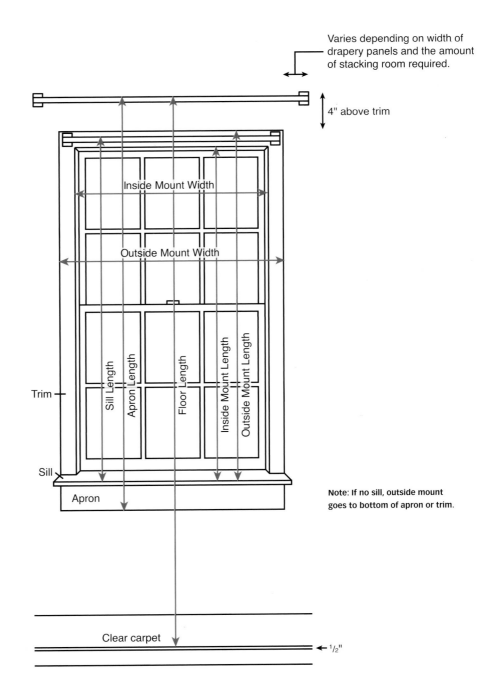

Varies depending on width of
drapery panels and the amount
of stacking room required.

4" above trim

Inside Mount Width

Outside Mount Width

Sill Length

Apron Length

Floor Length

Inside Mount Length

Outside Mount Length

Trim

Sill

Apron

Clear carpet

½"

**Note: If no sill, outside mount
goes to bottom of apron or trim.**

Cornice board

1 Decide on the placement of the cornice. It needs to cover the drapery tops and all hardware, and still allow for movement of the drapery and blinds. Measure the width of the window or the current window treatment. Add 2 inches on either side of the window. Add another 1½ inches to allow for the thickness of the 1x4 framing boards (¾ inch on each side). For example, if the window is 30 inches wide, you'll end up with a measurement of 35½ inches. Decide on the height of the cornice board. Cornice boards are usually mounted 4 inches above the top of the window frame or window treatment. The height of the cornice board is generally ⅓ of the total height measurement of the window or current window treatment.

2 Cut the 1x4 board to the width measurement determined in Step 1 for the frame top. **Note:** *Use the circular saw to make cuts, or ask your lumber dealer. Most will cut the wood for you if you provide the measurements. Some charge a small fee, but it is worth it if you do not want to invest in this type of saw.* Cut two 1x4 boards to the desired height for frame sides. Use finish nails to attach frame top to frame sides.

3 Measure the outside dimensions of the frame and cut a piece of plywood to this measurement (or have the lumberyard do it for you). Use finish nails to attach the plywood to the frame.

4 Unfold the quilt batting and smooth it out on the front of the frame. Gently fold the batting over the exposed frame side pieces to the reverse side.

From Shari

This was one of our very first *Room by Room* projects together. The cornices were for Matt's first apartment when he moved to Ohio and I think they were the start of something big!

Note: *Do not pull batting too tightly—it will stretch too much and lose the padded effect.* Staple the batting to the reverse side of the frame (not the exposed sides). Trim excess batting.

5 Attach fabric in the same manner as the batting. If the fabric has a distinct pattern, make sure the fabric stays straight on the frame. **Note:** *Begin stapling at the center of the frame and work out toward the ends. This makes it easier to keep the fabric straight and taut.*

6 Use drywall screws to attach the L-brackets to the wall at least 2 inches above the drapery rods to allow the draperies to be opened and closed without hindrance. Place the cornice board in position and attach the board to the secured L-brackets. This is a tight fit, but it is possible to reach your hand up and behind the cornice board, carefully balancing the screw in the bit of the drill. ■

TIP

For easier removal, attach the cornice board with triangular picture hanging hooks screwed right into the top of the frame. Place nails in the wall and hang. If you are concerned about the hooks showing, place the top 1x4 board about 1 inch down from the tops of the side pieces when you are assembling the frame. Be sure to attach the plywood facing even with the tops of the frame sides.

Whimsical Cloud Cornice Board

These cloud-shaped cornice boards are just right for a child's room (or anywhere you'd like a touch of lighthearted whimsy). The wispy quality comes from wrapping the board in quilt batting and soft terry cloth. An additional smaller cloud panel on the front of the larger one adds depth to this unique project.

Terry cloth

Quilt batting (cotton or polyester)

Homasote boards

¼-inch plywood

1x4 pine (use 1x6 or wider if cornice board will be placed over draperies)

Finish nails

3-inch L-brackets

1-inch and 1¼-inch drywall screws

MATERIALS ON HAND

Tape measure

Circular saw

Jigsaw or sharp utility knife

Staple gun with ⅜-inch staples

Cordless drill with Phillips bits

Pencil

Project notes

Read through the instructions for the Fabric-Covered Cornice Board on page 29 before beginning.

Available through building suppliers, lumberyards or large home-improvement stores, Homasote is made from recycled paper and newsprint that has been processed by pressure rollers and heat. The resulting light gray fiberboard is weather-resistant, insulating and extremely durable with 2–3 times the strength of light-density wood fiberboard.

Cornice board

1 Follow Steps 1-3 of Fabric-Covered Cornice Board on page 330 to determine size and construct frame.

2 Place the frame on the Homasote sheet. Use a pencil to sketch a cloud shape that completely covers the frame. Cut out the cloud shape with a jigsaw or a very sharp utility knife. *Optional: For added dimension, draw and cut a second smaller cloud shape to attach to the face of the larger cloud.*

3 Wrap the cloud shape(s) with quilt batting, stapling to the back. When wrapping, cover a few inches of the back to prevent the raw side of the Homasote from showing.

4 Wrap padded cloud shapes with terry cloth, stapling fabric on the reverse side as in Step 3.

5 Attach the small cloud to the front of the large cloud, using 1¼-inch drywall screws from the

reverse side of the larger cloud. Be careful not to drive screws through the front of the small cloud panel.

6 With the clouds facedown, position the cornice-box frame on the back side of the large cloud, making sure that the cornice frame does not protrude from the edges of the clouds. Attach the clouds to the cornice boxes using 1-inch drywall screws from the reverse side of the cornice box.

7 To attach the cornices to the wall, first attach the L-brackets to the wall 4 inches above the window or 2 inches above drapery rods. Place the cornice board in position, and from behind, screw through the L-bracket and into the top of the cornice. ∎

Other shapes are also possible with this type of cornice board. How about a row of cheerful sunflower blossoms cut from Homasote and then covered with felt? How about an apple tree? Cover the Homasote with green felt and attach red felt-covered apple shapes. Let your imagination go and enjoy the process as much as the results!

TIP

From Matt

If at all possible, cut the Homasote boards with a sharp utility knife, changing the blade often. Using a jigsaw results in tons of dust and lots of cleanup time. If you do use a saw, be sure to wear a particle mask.

Make Your Own Rag Roller!

Ragging a wall in the usual manner (dabbing paint-dipped rags on the surface of the wall) is a time-consuming and tiring process. This handy rag roller is easy to make and makes quick work of applying an interesting finish to a wall.

Prepare the walls

1 Start with a clean base coat on the walls. As long as the current paint is not peeling and is free of dirt and grease, it is not necessary to repaint.

2 Mask off the trim and ceiling edges with painter's tape.

Rag roller

1 To make the rag roller, use the pencil to divide the chamois into nine 3-inch squares. Cut out the squares with utility scissors, or a straightedge and a sharp knife.

2 Place a roller on the roller frame. Starting on the left edge, staple a chamois piece onto the roller. Be sure that the staple penetrates the roller cover. If the chamois piece seems loose, use another staple to secure it in place. Make sure the staples are flush with the cover to prevent tiny staple prints from transferring to the wall.

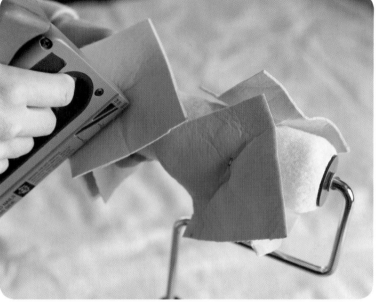

3 Repeat this process until you have three squares of chamois stapled to the length of the roller.

4 Spin the roller cover a third of a turn and repeat the stapling process with three more pieces of chamois, repositioning and rotating the chamois squares to create a random pattern.

5 Turn the roller another third of a turn and repeat process with remaining three squares of chamois.

From Matt
I find it helpful to rinse the rag roller after each wall. The chamois will become saturated, which diminishes the effect. For corners near the ceiling, cover your fingers with a small piece of chamois and dab paint into the corners. You may become a little dappled, but who said painters have to be neat?

Using your rag roller

1 To make the chamois more pliable and able to absorb paint, dampen the chamois with water. Don't oversaturate.

2 Gently roll the rag roller into the contrasting paint. The idea is to cover only the chamois with paint, not the roller cover. If the roller seems oversaturated, remove excess paint by rolling it off on brown paper bags or paper towels before applying paint to the wall.

3 Working on one wall at a time, beginning in the top left corner, rag-roll the paint on in 4-foot square areas, completing columns of color. Continue moving down the wall in this fashion, keeping a wet edge.

4 When the wall is finished, remove the painter's tape and continue around the room.

5 When the room is complete, wash the roller in cool water, squeezing excess paint out of the chamois squares. ∎

Ragging ON

This board shows a close-up view of ragging on, which is pictured in the guest bedroom. It is the process of adding paint to the rag roller and then rolling the wet roller onto the wall, leaving very defined fabric prints. For the bedroom walls we used an off-white base coat and two different colors to rag on.

Ragging OFF

This board demonstrates the more subtle look of ragging off. This process requires a dry base coat. Then tape off panels that look like strips of wallpaper. To apply the technique, a panel is coated with paint or glaze using a regular paint roller. Then, the rag-roller is rolled over the wet paint or glaze to remove the wet finish. The end result is a softer look with less contrast.

As with all paint techniques, test your selection of colors on a sample board. When finished, the base coat should show through in places, and the most prominent color will be the last coat applied.

TIP

Signature Projects Signature Projects
projects signature projects
nature projects signature projects

Picket Fence Headboard

A secret garden theme is so appropriate for a young girl's bedroom. This project is a replica of a picket fence front gate with a gently curving top and bottom. Who wouldn't want to dream under this garden gate?

Project note

Project instructions are for a double bed (54 inches wide). Increase width by adding boards to both ends of the headboard to maintain symmetry. The highest point is the center board (5 feet), gradually decreasing down to the end boards (4 feet).

Garden gate

1 For the pickets, cut 1x6 boards to seven 4 feet lengths. For the back supports, cut two 1x4 boards to 54 inches. Use a carpenter's square and circular saw to mark and make all cuts.

2 To duplicate the look of a picket, cut a curved or pointed top. Use a plastic coffee-can lid as a template for consistent curves. Draw the curve on all seven boards and cut out using a jigsaw. A scroll blade cuts fine smooth curves.

3 Sand all boards with a 120-grit sandpaper to remove pencil marks and any splinters. Choose the best-looking side of each board to be used for the front.

4 Before assembling the headboard, finish all the boards with a paint wash. Pour out a small amount of paint in a paint tray or old plastic bowl. Dip a rag or clean white sock in paint, squeeze out excess, then "wash" paint onto the front and sides of the headboard. Rub the boards in a circular motion along the grain—just like you'd wash a car. For a more translucent wash, dilute the paint with a small amount of water. Let dry.

5 Mark the center of a 1x4 back support (27 inches). Use this support board as a straightedge. Lay pickets on the floor with the reverse side facing up. Lay one picket at the center of the support board, 1 foot up from the

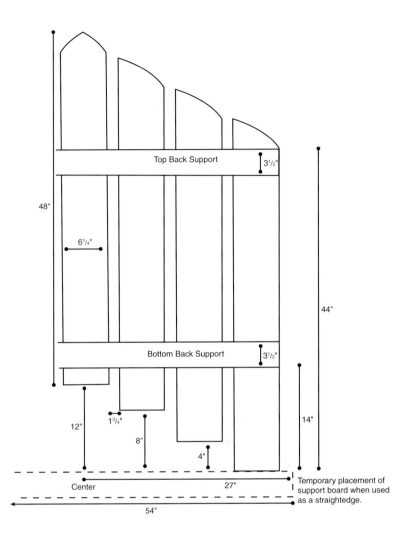

From Matt

Most lumberyards or do-it-yourself stores will crosscut lumber to the correct length. All you have to do is ask! If you are using a circular saw to cut the boards to length yourself, try using a roofer's speed square as a guide for the circular blade. The speed square has a lip that rests against the edge of the board, making a perfect guide for the saw.

straightedge. Using the center picket as a guide, measure down 4 inches from the top of the board and place the next two pickets at that height, one on either side, spacing them 1¾ inches apart. Measure down another 4 inches from the second set of boards and add another two pickets at this height. Repeat once more for the last set of pickets (the bottom of these pickets should be level with the straightedge).

6 When the pickets are in position, place a support board horizontally across all the pickets so that the top of the support is 4 inches below the top of the end or lowest picket (44 inches from the floor). Place the bottom support board horizontally across the pickets, 14 inches from the bottom of the end pickets.

7 Attach the support boards to the pickets, using 2 drywall screws in each headboard board. Before tightening, make sure all boards are square.

8 At this point, the headboard can be attached to the wall behind the bed using self-anchoring molly bolts and 2-inch drywall screws, drilling through the support boards. To attach the headboard to the metal bed frame, drill holes through the end pickets to line up with the holes in the bed frame. Use machine bolts, washers and nuts to hold the headboard in place. ■

We decided not to finish the headboard any further than the paint wash, but here are some other options:

TIPS

After applying the paint wash, seal the headboard with polyurethane. This helps when dusting and allows the headboard to be wiped off with a soft cloth and water. Keep in mind that the polyurethane will add a sheen.

Instead of applying a paint wash, simply prime the headboard with a multipurpose sealer.

The washing technique doesn't get the wood wet enough to raise the grain. If you prime the wood pieces the boards will need to be sanded when dry, using a 220-grit sandpaper. Sand it and paint with the color of your choice.

How To Paint a Picket Fence on the Walls

The only project in this room that is just as cute as the picket fence headboard, is the painted picket fence on the surrounding walls. It makes the headboard look like it is a gate to the world of dreams! Painting the fence is easy. Grab the curved template used to round the top of the center picket and position it on the wall to match the height of the lowest part of the headboard. Use a long level and create a very light pencil line at this height. Trace around the template as you move it around the room, leaving 1 inch between pickets. Use 1 inch blue painter's tape to mask off the space between the pickets. Paint in the fence, cutting in around the picket top with a small sash brush. Then roll the rest of the fence if you wish. In order for the whole fence to look hand-painted, lay off the entire wall of pickets with vertical brushstrokes. Remove the tape and enjoy!

Baby's Name

Birthdate

Weight   Length

Apple Tree Mural

Faraway places, fantastic creatures and imaginary friends are all within reach if you are equipped with paintbrushes, stamps, stencils and a little imagination. If you're looking for something really different for your home, consider a painted mural!

SHOPPING LIST

Greeting card, fabric or photo for inspiration

Paint in desired colors

Stencils and/or foam stamps to duplicate motifs

1-inch latex sash paintbrushes

Foam brushes

Artist brushes (for detail work)

MATERIALS ON HAND

Level

Drop cloth

Painter's tape

Paper towels

Pencil

Project note

To prevent cracking, make sure each coat of paint has a chance to dry completely before applying a new layer of color. Putting wet paint over damp paint that has filmed over is what causes cracking and peeling of the new layers.

1 Choose a greeting card, printed fabric or photo from a book or magazine to use as the mural inspiration. Spend some time with this inspiration piece.

Determine how to create what you see. Repeated motifs such as apples and leaves can often be created by using purchased foam stamps. Something more architectural, such as a fence, columns or windows, can be created using stencils found in your local craft store. Consider the materials you need to create the desired results, and gather them up.

2 Determine the painting order. If your design includes a sky and trees, for example, it is easier to paint the upper wall blue for the sky first, and then add the trees, than it is to paint the trees and then try to fill in the sky around them. In this mural,

the fence is the dominant element. We determined the height, then painted the blue sky on each of the walls. We thought the spaces between the pickets on the fence looked fine in the sky color. When the blue paint dried, we penciled in and taped off the fence using a level and painter's tape. We left room for the quilt hanging over the fence by taping off that area as well. Next we painted the trees and added the apples using a foam stamp. Some of the details were hand-drawn,

such as the bunny weathervane that we added, using our greeting-card artwork as a guide.

3 Now add the details, such as outlining fence posts with black paint pens, painting shadows in soft gray, and adding dimension with details such as the wooden birdhouse we cut in half to hang from the trees. This is where the mural comes to life, and the more detail you add, the more amazing your mural creation becomes. ■

From Shari

Clear your calendar upon completion of your mural masterpiece. Once everyone in your familiy sees yours, they are going to want you to paint a fantasy room in their homes!

This lovely tree continues up a full two stories. Only three latex paint colors were used; they are just used heavier in some areas, lighter in others. The plain white background is an integral part of the tree. Make sure you have the right ladder for this project; otherwise, hire a professional!

Sometimes you just have to be an artist to create a mural. This one was painted by Jennifer, one of our designers. She can paint anything, and Matt and I both appreciate her artistic talent.

This mural was inspired by a few prints I found for this nursery. We started with yellow walls and added a few puffy clouds with white paint and a paint-washing technique. When the clouds were dry, we drew the balloons by tying a pencil to a string with a push pin on one end to create a large compass, which we used to draw the circles. The baskets and details were penciled in by hand, although we did use a straightedge to draw the rope lines from the balloons to the baskets.

Painting a mural can take quite a bit of time. Do not plan on using the room while painting, so that you can leave drop cloths and mural materials in place until the project is finished.

TIP

This was our first mural, which was super-easy to create. I just drew simple pencil lines for the trunks, and traced around a cardboard cutout shape of a palm-leaf frond, which I placed on the wall and traced over and over again. Since this was a first mural project, I didn't add any shading or shadows for detailing, but it still looks great!

BACKGROUND PROJECTS

The walls and ceiling of a room set the stage for your decor and your life. Make sure they are cheery, uplifting and reflect who you are or want to be. The ideas are limited only by your imagination. While you are thinking, here are a few ideas just to get you started!

Faux Beams

Turn an ordinary ceiling into something extraordinary with the addition of faux beams. This isn't a project for the faint of heart—it requires some work, skill and, above all, a sense of adventure. The spectacular results will enhance your living spaces for years to come.

Project notes

This project requires two people to complete—one to lift the beam sections and a second person to attach the sections to the ceiling.

Instructions are written for beams that measure approximately 4 inches high and 8 inches wide. Beams can be made narrower or wider depending on the width of lumber chosen.

Steps

1 Measure the room and determine the finished size of the beam. Purchase enough lumber to make the desired number of beams.

2 Determine the placement of the beams. Divide the ceiling so that there will be equal distance between the beams. Lay out the location of each beam by using a carpenter's square placed against the wall to make sure that the beam placement is square, and a laser level to lay out the line, marking the placement of the beam with a pencil. The straighter the line, the better the final results.

3 Cut mounting blocks from the 2x4 lumber the inside width of the beam. This is the measurement of the width of the bottom board. You will need at least 4 blocks for every 10 feet of beam.

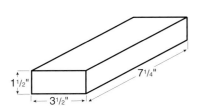

Fig. 1
Mounting Block

4 Drill pilot holes into the blocks for the toggle bolts.

5 Mark block placement on the ceiling by pushing an awl through the pilot holes into the ceiling. Blocks should be placed at each end of the beam and evenly spaced along the beam line, perpendicular to the beam lines. Drill pilot holes into the ceiling at the marked locations. Use toggle bolts to attach the mounting blocks.

6 Cut the side pieces of the beam to length, using the miter saw. For long beams, use several sections for the run of the beam and miter the ends of the side pieces to create a clean joint. The beams in the photo on the facing page are constructed with two pieces of 1x4 per side.

7 Attach the side pieces to the blocks using a nail gun. If more than one side piece is used, make sure that a mounting block is located where the two side pieces will be joined.

8 Cut the bottom board to length. Again, more than one piece may be necessary for long beams. If more than one bottom piece is used, miter the ends of the cut where the two will meet to make a smoother joint.

9 Hold the bottom in place and secure to the side pieces with the nail gun, referring to Fig. 2.

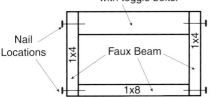

Mounting block attached to ceiling with toggle bolts.

Nail Locations

1x4   Faux Beam   1x4

1x8

Fig. 2
Cross Section of Faux Beam

10 Use decorative edge molding along the side pieces to add finish detail and to cover any gaps between the ceiling and the beam. Cut to length and install with the nail gun (see small photo on page 48).

11 Paint and finish the beam in the desired color and technique. ∎

From Matt
Basically, you are creating a long 3-sided box that will be installed on the ceiling. If you are lucky enough to find the ceiling joists and can secure the 2x4 mounting blocks to them, that would be great, but it seems like that never happens. Just make sure that you have enough blocks per beam and that there is always a block where joints meet.

Fabric-Covered Ceiling

Fabric is the perfect material for so many things, but have you ever considered using it on the ceiling? It certainly becomes an unexpected touch in any room, and the softness adds a warmth and texture that a painted ceiling just doesn't have.

Project note

This is definitely a project that requires a friend to help. Also, think about the size of the ceiling you are covering. For your first attempt, make sure the ceiling is a simple square or rectangle and that it isn't much wider than 8 feet, since longer lengths of fabric can be very cumbersome to work with.

Steps

1 Measure the ceiling and determine the amount of fabric needed, keeping in mind that several inches of the width of the fabric are needed to wrap onto the battens. The ceiling in the photograph required four panels to fill the length of the room.

2 Cut the battens to the width of the room. Also cut the fabric panels to the width of the room, adding approximately 6 inches to wrap down onto the walls. Cut several panels before beginning.

3 Start at the shortest end of the room and work along the length of the room. Lay the first panel on the floor against the short wall with the wrong side of the fabric facing up. Lay the first batten against the selvage edge of the fabric nearest the wall. Wrap the selvage up and around the batten and staple it in place.

4 Lift the batten and fabric straight up to the corner where the ceiling meets the wall. The fabric will fall straight down against the wall. Screw the batten to the ceiling.

> *From Shari*
> Although this project requires more than one person, it really is fairly easy and has very high impact. Your friends and family will love it!

5 Lift the other selvage edge of fabric up to the ceiling and pull it taut. Staple this edge directly to the ceiling, working from the middle and then out to the wall edges to eliminate the wrinkles.

6 The short ends of fabric will wrap slightly onto the wall. Staple these short ends to the wall and trim excess fabric.

7 Continue this process, overlapping the next batten over the stapled selvage edge of the previous panel, until the ceiling is completely covered. The very last panel is wrapped onto the end wall and stapled to the wall close to the ceiling.

8 To finish the tops of the walls, create a paper template to make scallops from additional strips of fabric. Iron interfacing on the back of the strips following manufacturer's instructions. Trace around the template and cut out the scalloped strips. Attach trim with hot glue to finish off the edges of the scallops. Fold 1 inch of fabric along long straight edges to wrong side and press in place.

9 Staple the turned-under hem of the scalloped strips to the wall where it meets the ceiling. ∎

> **The best way to hold the scallop in place** is to hot glue an upholsterer's cardboard tacking strip along the crease of the 1-inch turned-under hem. **TIP**

Painted Paneling

Don't let a dark paneled room hold you back from enjoying one of your favorite spaces. Paneling can easily be painted and the transformation will completely change the way you feel about your room!

Project note

Use a satin-finish latex paint for durability and easier cleaning.

Steps

1 Wash the paneling with liquid dish soap. Rinse well. Allow to dry thoroughly.

2 Sand cleaned paneling with a 220-grit sandpaper attached to a pole sander. Be sure to remove shine from high-gloss polyurethane coatings.

3 Prime the paneling with a stain-blocking primer, making sure to mask off the ceiling, trim and baseboard. Cut in the edges with a brush and roll the primer on the rest of the wall. Allow to dry for at least 24 hours.

4 With latex paint, cut in the edges of the wall with a brush. Roll the paint on the rest of the wall. Let dry for 24 hours, and then roll on a second coat of paint. ∎

> **After you've rolled a small section** of the wall with the latex paint, use a 4-inch-wide brush to go over the wall from ceiling to floor in long strokes. Brush strokes enhance the wood grain—remember, all walls were painted with brushes before rollers were invented!
>
> **TIP**

From Matt

There are many types of paneling out there. Some are real wood with real grooves and, believe it or not, some types of paneling are just photographs of wood laminated to a backing. If yours is the photo type, there is no need for sanding, but priming is critical. Test by trying to scratch off the top layer. If it won't come off, do a little sanding.

Starched Fabric Wallcovering

If you enjoy the look of wall covering on your walls, but are looking for something more unusual, and easier to remove if needed, then you must try starching fabric to your walls.

SHOPPING LIST

Medium-weight designer fabric of your choice

Gallons of starch

MATERIALS ON HAND

Step stool, if needed

Drop cloths

Roller frame and ⅜-inch roller cover

Paint tray and liner

Long level

Pencil

Scissors

Pushpins

Straightedge

Utility knife and extra blades

Sponge

Wallpaper brush

Project note

Use plastic-lined paper drop cloths to absorb the drips from the starch. These may have to be changed at every new wall.

Base

1 Start by measuring the full width of the fabric, including the selvage edges. Then go to the first corner on the wall, and measure out the full width of the fabric, minus the width of one selvage edge; draw a light vertical level line.

2 Measure the length of the cuts of fabric you will need, calculating any pattern matching and leaving enough extra at the top and bottom to trim off. Cut several lengths of fabric and set to the side. This will speed the process along once you begin starching.

3 Prepare the work area by laying down drop cloths, tight to the wall. Have the wallpaper brush, pushpins, sponge, straightedge and utility knife ready to go. Pour starch into the paint tray liner and load up the roller.

4 Roll the starch on the wall in the area of the first panel. Be generous with the starch. Quickly grab the first piece of fabric, and place it on the wall with the selvage edge lined up against the level line. The starch will start soaking into the fabric and begin holding it to the wall. If this isn't happening right away, use pushpins to hold the fabric in place at the corners along the top. The wallpaper brush will help in the smoothing of the fabric.

5 Once the fabric is level and positioned correctly, load up the roller and roll starch over the top of the fabric soaking it well in all areas, without creating too much drippage.

6 Use the sponge to wipe off the excess starch, remove the pushpins, and trim off the excess fabric at the top and bottom using the straightedge and a fresh, sharp blade.

7 The second piece of fabric goes up just the same way, only the left selvage of the fabric will overlap past the right selvage of the first panel. This is done so a cut can be made between the two to leave a perfectly butted seam.

When selecting your fabric, keep in mind that larger patterns take a lot more fabric and are harder to match, and that stripes have a tendency to start leaning. Just ask Matt; he solved this problem by shoving a buffet in front of some stripes that were a bit askew.

TIP

8 Once the cut is done, remove the selvage from the second panel, then lift the edge of the second panel to pull out the selvage of the first. Smooth the edges back down, adding starch with the roller if necessary, wipe clean and continue. **Note:** *Another method is to fold the selvage edge of the second panel under and press that edge against the wall, covering the first selvage edge to keep the knife from scoring the drywall.*

9 When going around corners, it's usually best to cut the last piece of fabric about ½–1 inch around the corner. Then, measure how much fabric is left and draw a vertical line at that exact measurement from the corner of the second wall.

10 Overlap the rest of the panel, butting it to the corner. True, the pattern won't match here, but it's difficult to keep a level vertical line when wrapping around corners.

11 Continue in this fashion until all your walls are complete, then marvel at the beautiful, textural addition you've made to your room! ∎

From Shari

The best part about this wall technique is that when it does come time to take the fabric down and try something new … it peels off the wall like a dream! You'll only need to wash the wall to remove the starch.

Painted Faux-Tile Backsplash

Nothing can give your kitchen cabinets more pizzazz than a painted faux-tile backsplash. It adds color, depth and a totally customized look—and half the beauty is that you created it yourself!

Project note

Quarter-inch-wide masking tape can be difficult to find. Try a craft store or a quilting shop in your area. When we can't find it, we have resorted to using a sharp utility knife to cut wider tape down to size while it is still on the roll. This can be tricky, so be careful not to cut yourself.

Before you begin

Start by determining the size and shape of your tiles. Will they be rectangular? square? octagonal? Next determine how your design will be placed in the backsplash. Is there enough room for an even number of tiles or do you need to border your design with an additional line of small mosaics or bar-shaped tiles?

Determine if the color of the backsplash will be the grout color. If not, paint a base coat of desired grout color to cover the entire backsplash; let dry.

Steps

1 Draw the tile layout on the backsplash, using the measuring tape, level and pencil. When you draw a line for the ¼-inch-wide masking tape, draw only one and make it a habit to always place the tape on one side or the other so you can hide the line when you paint the tile.

With painter's blue tape, mask off the countertop, the base of the upper cabinets, and any side walls that are not being tiled.

2 Apply the ¼-inch-wide masking tape to the predetermined side of the pencil lines. Make sure to use your thumbnail or the back of a spoon to run along the edges of the tape to prevent paint seepage, which will ruin the crisp edges of the grout.

3 Now that all the tape is up, it's time to start painting the tiles. For one of our projects we used several colors selected from a painted vase in the room. Since we wanted to spread the colors randomly, we started with the darkest, since it would show up the most, and began painting tiles with a foam brush. We then stood in the middle of the room to look around and take in as much of the backsplash as possible to make sure the color placement looked random.

4 Continue in this fashion, adding one color after the other. Keep the brushes wet for all colors—you may have to go back to a previously used color to fill in an area to make it look balanced.

5 As soon as an area is filled in, remove the ¼-inch-wide masking tape to keep the paint film from drying over the tape and lifting when the tape is removed. Remove the tape slowly to prevent lifting the paint.

6 When the tiles are painted and dry, it's time to give them some dimension. This is accomplished through the use of the two tones of glaze. First, determine the direction of the

strongest light source in the room. If it is a double patio door, or a large window, consider the location and where it is compared to the tile. If the light in the room is coming from the right of the tiles, then the white or cream glaze will be brushed on from the right side and from the top. The brown glaze will be brushed on the tiles from the left side and then up from the bottom. Make sure to paint the brown glaze highlights first and the white or cream second. These barely there highlights will really make your tiles come to life. Remember to use a very light touch so as not to cover the color of the tile, just highlight it.

7 The final step is to add a coat of polyurethane to the entire backsplash. This will make it easier to clean up than real tile since the grout is generally not protected! ∎

From Shari

For a vintage or old-world effect, use a washing technique to age painted tiles. Or use a stencil or a stamp to add veggies, teapots, roosters or other images to a few tiles in the arrangement. Remember, this is a totally one-of-a-kind design—take the time to really make it yours.

Bead-Board Paneling

Bead-board paneling brings to mind beach cottages and country-style decorating. Panels are available in standard 4x8-foot sections, making them perfect for everything from creating wainscoting to covering a wall from top to bottom.

Project notes

Whether you paint or stain the panels, make sure to leave the paneling sheets in the room where they will be installed for at least 48 hours. This allows them to acclimatize to the room's humidity, reducing the effects of expansion and contraction.

If you plan to stain the paneling, work in a well-ventilated garage to eliminate the risk of spilling stain on carpeting or floors. Stain the paneling a few days before you plan to install it to allow it to dry thoroughly.

Before you begin

Prepare the wall by removing all outlet and switch-plate covers. The baseboard should also be removed if you plan to install a new one. If you are not changing the existing baseboard, do not remove it.

You may either install the paneling all the way to the ceiling line or only cover half or three quarters of the wall. Whatever you decide, the installation method is the same. If the paneling will only cover a portion of the wall, you will also need to select a cap molding for along the top edge. The instructions that follow are for installing 6-foot-high paneling.

Steps

1 Using a long level and a tape measure, place a level horizontal line on each wall around the room at a 6-foot height.

2 Use a stud finder to locate the studs along the level line and mark them above the 6-foot height with small pieces of painter's tape. Most studs are placed 16 inches apart.

3 Cut the bead-board paneling into 6-foot lengths. **Note:** *When using a circular saw on paneling, be sure to cut it with the beaded side facing down. This will prevent tearing the paneling due to the rotation of the saw blade.*

When you need to cut out for a switch plate or outlet, take

measurements and locate its position on the back of the paneling. (Double check all of these measurements and markings since the back is the mirror image.) Use a drill bit to start a hole, then use the jigsaw to cut out the opening.

4 Dry-fit the paneling: Place the cut paneling in position to be sure it fits. If this is the first panel, make sure the piece is placed in the corner, and then set a level on the outer edge away from the corner. Make sure the panel is plumb, and draw a reference line along that edge. You will repeat this process at every corner of the room.

5 Use the caulking gun to apply paneling adhesive to the back of the sheet in zigzag lines to give ample surface coverage. Make sure edges have enough adhesive, but not so much that adhesive will ooze out when paneling is applied. Using reference lines as a guide,

place paneling in position and press against the wall with your hands.

6 Secure paneling to the wall with paneling nails at the previously marked studs. Make sure you nail into the studs. Evenly space the nails and be consistent in placement for a more attractive appearance.

7 When you reach a corner, dry-fit the last piece of paneling by flipping it over and placing the right side against the wall. Mark where the last-installed panel falls at the top and bottom of the new piece. Draw a line connecting both points and cut along this line. The last panel should fit evenly, even if the corner is out of square. Continue in this fashion around the entire room.

8 To finish off the top of the paneling, measure and install cap molding. Using a nail gun eliminates the need to drill pilot holes to use with standard finishing nails. ∎

From Matt

You will probably need to use switch and outlet spacers to bring your electrical to the surface of the new paneling. Follow the manufacturer's instructions so the switch plates and outlet covers fit correctly. As always, turn off the electricity at the main box before starting!

To help hide the gap created when the paneling contracts, paint the wall behind the paneling in a color that matches the paint or stain of the paneling.

Color Blocking

Color blocking is a great technique to use when you are looking for a unique background treatment for a room. Bold and extreme, or soft and ethereal, the technique itself is easy to execute. The challenge comes in the selection of the colors.

Project note

When you go to the paint store to select your colors, remember to bring something from the room, such as an arm cap from a sofa or patterned chair. You need to have something with you as a guide so you know what families of color to select.

Steps

1 Start with the wall to be painted with the lightest color, tape off the baseboards, add the drop cloths, cut in at the corner of the wall and ceiling, and a few feet along the baseboard. Begin rolling on the new color.

2 When you have rolled up to the cut-in lines, cut in a few more feet at the ceiling and floor, and then fill in with the roller.

3 Continue in this fashion until the first wall is complete; remove tape before paint dries.

4 Move across the room to the opposite wall and follow Steps 1–3 using a different paint color. Repeat for the remainder of the walls, waiting until the edges in the corners are dry before continuing. ∎

From Shari

Selecting just the right colors is the most difficult part of this project. We've used this technique several times and have relied on the experts to give us our color advice. For instance, in the cream, gold, celery green and aqua room shown on page 62, we selected colors that matched a watercolor painting used above the fireplace. We loved the painting, so why not apply those colors to the walls! And here's another tip, if you stay within the same value (how light or dark a color is) and the same saturation (how bright or neutral a color is), it keeps the combination of hues more appealing.

The orange wall is the first wall you see as you enter this teen's bedroom. Because it is the brightest of the colors selected, it seems to advance into the room, making a stronger statement. Having the bedding in solid colors as well makes the orange wall act almost as a headboard!

Selecting three instead of four different colors helps create a more cohesive statement, especially since the colors are so bold. With navy on the two end walls, the orange can be dominant, and the olive is calmer—perfect for the study area of the room.

Paper-Covered Vent & Switch-Plate Cover

Decorating is all about the details. After spending hours installing wallpaper, nothing can spoil the results quicker than unsightly cold-air returns and switch-plate covers. However, with a small investment of time, you can make them virtually disappear by covering them with matching wallpaper.

Project note

Change the blade of the utility knife frequently to cut through the wet wallpaper without tearing it.

Steps

1 Remove the vent and give it a thorough cleaning; rinse well and dry. Scuff the finish with a light sanding using 220-grit sandpaper or steel wool.

2 Cut a piece of paper 2 inches larger all the way around than the vent. Just hold up a section of wallpaper until you find the matching pattern, and then cut out enough to cover the vent or plate. Apply wallpaper paste to the paper and place the paper on the front of the vent, smoothing it down and positioning it to match the wall.

3 From the front of the vent, use the sharp utility knife to score through the paper along the ridges created by the strips of metal that make up the vent. As you cut, press the paper to the metal strips, completely covering them.

4 When all the metal strips are covered, turn over the vent and reapply wallpaper paste if necessary around the edge of the paper. Fold the paper to the back of the vent and press to hold in place.

5 Allow the wallpaper to dry on the vent before reinstalling it in the wall.

Use the same technique to cover switch plates and outlet covers with wallpaper. ∎

From Shari

Since this project is all about the details, make sure the covered vent or switch-plate cover matches perfectly with the wallpaper behind it. Just hold up a section of wallpaper until you find the matching pattern, and then cut out enough to cover the vent or plate.

If you are a stickler for details, like me, touch up the screw heads with matching paint!

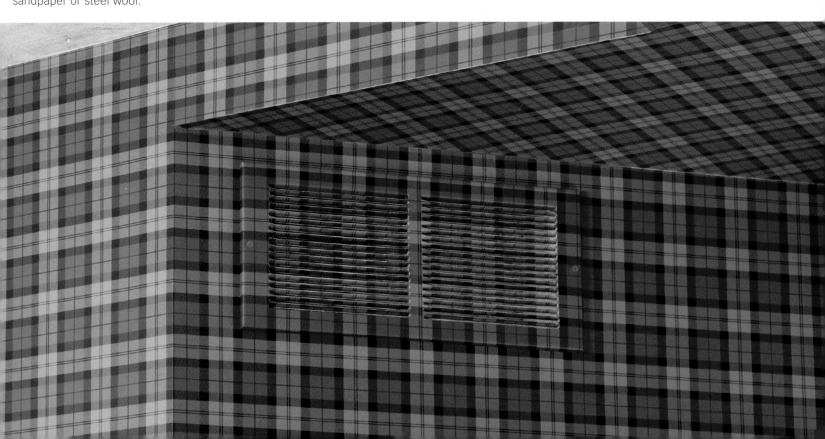

Stripes & Flowers

Add the look of expensive wallpaper to your home at a fraction of the cost. Paint, glaze and some imagination on your part make it easy and affordable.

Steps

1 Apply light yellow base coat to wall and allow to dry. Use a pencil and level to mark off 1¼-inch stripes spaced every 8 inches.

2 Use painter's blue tape to tape off stripes; paint stripes with ivory latex paint. Remove the tape before the paint dries. Allow the stripes to dry overnight before starting the glazing process.

3 To prepare for glazing, tape off panels measuring 24–32 inches, coinciding with the wide stripes. This will give the effect of wallpaper strips. Tape off every other panel. You'll be technique painting in every other one, and then will go back and fill in alternating panels.

4 Roll the glaze over a panel. Immediately pull the 4-inch flat-edge brush vertically down through the glaze on the entire panel, and then very gently pull the brush across horizontally so as not to cover up the vertical lines just created. Repeat on every other panel, removing the tape as you finish, and let dry.

Repeat procedure on remaining alternating panels.

5 For vines and flowers, use green paint and artist paintbrush to add a small wavy freehand line along one side of each of the white stripes. Add small strokes of green paint here and there to create leaves and add flower-bud details to the design with single dots of burgundy paint. Let dry. ∎

Let your imagination run wild with this technique. Paint diamonds in the stripes for a masculine look. Stamp the flowers if you are uncomfortable with a freehand technique. Or just stop with the stripes—this is a great look all by itself.

TIP

From Shari

I love this wall technique. Sure, it took a lot of steps, but it transformed a bathroom that really needed a full remodel into a room that looked like a million bucks for the cost of about $100.

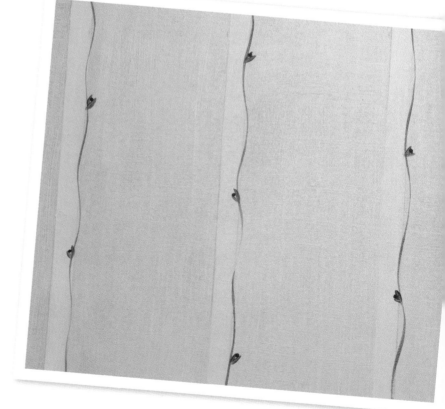

Bubble Painting

Try adapting one of your child's favorite pastimes into room decor by creating walls full of bright, happy bubbles. It's like taking a bubble bath all day long!

SHOPPING LIST

Circle templates or stencils

Stencil brushes in various sizes

Several shades of stencil cream in one color family

Painter's blue tape

MATERIALS ON HAND

Drop cloth

Project note

This technique takes a full day or two to complete. Remember that larger circles take up more space than smaller ones and can help move the project along faster.

Steps

1 Make sure the background paint is in good shape—clean and ready to be painted over.

2 Apply painter's blue tape to protect the chair rail and/or baseboards. Place a drop cloth on the floor to create a staging area for the paint and to protect the flooring.

3 Starting with the largest circle, and the lightest color paint, place the stencil or template against the wall and, while holding it with one hand, swirl the stencil paint in the circle opening until desired coverage is achieved.

4 Continue in this fashion around the entire room, filling in more bubbles at the bottom of the wall and fewer as the wall approaches the ceiling.

5 Select a smaller circle and continue with the lightest color until you are satisfied that you have enough of that color bubble on the wall.

6 Move on to darker paint colors and vary the size of the bubbles with them as well, until the room is filled to the brim with bubbles! ∎

Clean the stencil or template when the paint builds up around the edges. This will help keep the edges of the bubbles crisp and well-defined.

TIP

From Shari

If at all possible, get a friend to help. It will make the time go faster—and aren't projects just a little bit more fun when you are doing them with a friend?

Leaning Painted Panels

For rooms where painting may not be an option, or for something that is unique and can be considered a piece of decorative art, these leaning panels are a snap to make, and they add color and texture to any room.

Project note

When you go to the paint store to select colors make sure that you take something with you from the room, such as a fabric arm cap from a chair or a piece of art with background colors in the room.

Steps

1 Build the frame, using the miter saw to cut the 1x2 lumber to the desired length. (For the frames in the photo, the dimensions are 42 inches wide by 72 inches high). Mark and drill pilot holes for the corner braces. Assemble the pieces by attaching a brace in each corner and securing with screws.

2 Cut the drop cloth so that it overhangs the frame by at least 2 inches. Iron the drop cloth to eliminate any wrinkles. **Note:** *There is no need to wash the drop cloth—that will only create more wrinkles.*

3 Staple the fabric to the frame by laying the frame onto the fabric and pulling the fabric over the frame. Work from the center of the frame to the end. Staple

at least every 2 inches to secure the fabric. At the corners, cut and staple the fabric as if you are wrapping a gift. You may need to tap in the staples with a hammer to make sure that they are secure.

4 Paint the fabric using a 4-inch-wide paintbrush. For the project shown, we used a variety of colors and blended them together while the paint was still wet, working from the bottom up. ∎

From Matt

These panels certainly could be hung on the wall like painted canvases, but part of their charm is that they can be moved around at any time and placed in different locations in the room. Make several and set them up vertically or horizontally.

Painted Garage Floor

The garage is probably one of the least talked about rooms when it comes to decorating. Set the tone for your home by spiffing up the garage floor with a painted design that will welcome you home in style.

Before you begin

Preparation of a concrete garage floor is critical in order for the paint to adhere. Sweep the floor with a stiff-bristle broom to remove all the dust and debris. Hose down the floor to remove even more dust.

Lift any oil stains on the floor with clay cat litter. Allow the litter to sit on the stain overnight, and sweep it up and dispose of it properly.

If the litter does not remove the oil stain, wash the floor with a concentrated garage-floor cleaner. Use a stiff-bristle scrub brush and repeat a few times to lighten stain.

Oil stains can be particularly stubborn. If stains still remain after scrubbing, it may be necessary to clean the floor with a muriatic acid solution. Muriatic acid is extremely caustic and emits fumes that can be toxic if inhaled. It is necessary to wear old clothing, heavy gloves and a respirator before mixing or using this chemical. Pour muriatic acid into a pump-style garden sprayer and soak the stained areas. Use a stiff-bristle push broom to scrub the solution into the stain. Rinse with water and repeat if necessary. Dispose of the acid solution according to manufacturer's instructions.

At this point, rinse the entire floor again and let dry.

Steps

1 Mix the main color of the epoxy paint as directed by the manufacturer. Apply the paint with a brush and a roller using the same technique you would if you were painting a wall. You may need to apply more than one coat to cover. Let dry overnight between coats.

2 Use a long level to lay out and pencil in a border design. Tape off the inside border area. Mix a contrasting color of paint and apply using a roller. Remove the tape before the paint dries to eliminate the possibility of removing the paint with the tape.

3 If additional borders are desired, repeat Step 2, allowing the previous color to dry overnight. ■

From Matt

Many people do not paint their garage floors because they are concerned about the paint lifting off. This is actually caused by driving on the floor with hot tires. The hot tires pick up the paint and ruin the finish. Paint manufacturers have now formulated many types of paint that can resist some hot-tire pick up. Sometimes these paints do fail, but more often it is because the floor was not properly prepared. Careful cleaning of the floor, including removal of oil stains, will go a long way toward preventing a ruined floor. For even more protection, park your car on a purchased garage floor mat that cleans up easily. I do, and my painted floor still looks brand new!

SHOP PROJECTS

To people who love their shops, the project itself doesn't matter as much as the fact that there is a project. So select any one of many that are here, and if it's something you don't need, we're sure someone you know will!

Oak Bookcase

Create a handy storage piece that is custom-sized to fit behind your sofa. The optional rope lights add accent lighting and showcase display objects placed on the shelves.

Project size
72 inches W x 9¼ inches D x 34 inches H

Project note

Model project is constructed to fit behind a sofa 36 inches high and approximately 84 inches long. Adjust measurements as necessary to fit a sofa of other dimensions.

Frames & shelves

1 From 1x8 oak, cut two sides (A) to 33¼ inches and two shelves (B) to 68½ inches. Use wood glue and a nail gun to secure the two sides (A) to the bottom shelf (B) with outside edges flush and top of shelf 4 inches from bottoms of sides; secure the center shelf (B) midway between the bottom shelf and the tops of the sides.

Trim

1 From 1x2s, cut two 70-inch-long trim pieces (C) to fit across the top and bottom of the bookcase, flush with the outside edges. Attach bottom trim piece flush with the top of the bottom shelf (B); attach top trim piece flush with the tops of the sides (A).

2 Cut two 31-inch trim pieces (D) to cover the fronts of the sides (A) between the top and bottom trim pieces (C). Attach side trim pieces (D) flush with the outside edges, and butted into top and bottom trim pieces (C). Cut another 67-inch-long trim piece (E) to cover the front of the center shelf (B) between the side trim pieces. Attach center trim piece (E) flush with the top of the center shelf and butted into the side trim pieces (D).

Base

1 For base front (F), measure the front of the bookcase and cut a 1x4 to this length, mitered at both ends, so the short points line up with the case front (70 inches). Attach base front to the front of the bookcase with bottom edges flush with the bottom edges of the sides.

2 For side base pieces (G), measure from the back of the case to the long point of the front base and cut two 1x4s to this length (8 inches), each mitered on one end to match the front base and square on the other end. Attach to the case and the front base. These will add additional height and give dimension to the bookcase. *Optional: If desired, add interest to the trim before installing it by drawing a slight curve along the bottom of the front 1x4. Cut out the curve with a jigsaw.*

Back & top

1 Cut a ¼-inch piece of oak plywood 33¼ inches tall by 69½ inches wide to fit the back of the bookcase (H), excluding the base pieces. Use the nail gun to attach this piece to sides.

2 Using the 1x10x72-inch oak board for the top (I), position the top flush with back of bookcase and centered side to side; secure with 2-inch L-brackets and ¾-inch screws. *Note: Attach brackets to the insides of sides (A) first, then to the top from below.*

Finishing

1 Sand the entire bookcase and remove the dust. Finish as desired.

Optional: Attach a string of rope lights to the 1x2s on the top and center shelves to highlight books and accessories, and to add accent lighting. ∎

If you paint this project, fill and sand all nail holes before priming and painting. If you stain the bookcase, stain first and allow to dry. Fill in the nail holes with matching wood putty. **TIP**

From Matt

The addition of rope lighting is a neat effect. String the lights underneath the top and center shelves. The lights will be hidden by the 1x2 trim pieces. Use a 1½-inch spade bit to drill a hole in the back of the bookcase for the plug and wire to fit through. When you drill a hole of this size with a spade bit, drill halfway through from one side, then remove the bit and drill the rest of the way through from the opposite side to prevent tearing the wood.

OAK BOOKCASE
(Actual Sizes)

P	T	W	L	#
A	¾"	7¼"	33¼"	2
B	¾"	7¼"	68½"	2
C	¾"	1½"	70"	2
D	¾"	1½"	31"	2
E	¾"	1½"	67"	1
F	¾"	3½"	71½"	1
G	¾"	3½"	8"	2
H	¼"	33¼"	69½"	1
I	¾"	9¼"	72"	1

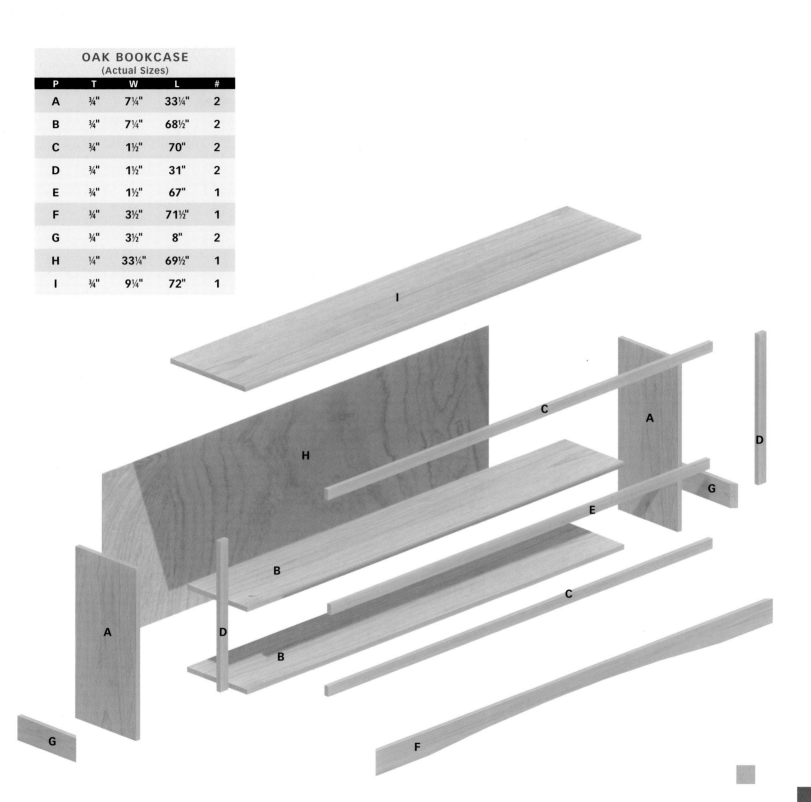

Open-Front Cabinet

This simple, yet handsome cabinet is the perfect piece of furniture for a family room or den. Built with pine, the cabinet can be a storage piece for books, collectibles and a television. This is a great project for an autumn weekend.

Project size

43 inches W x 23 inches D x
80 inches H

From Matt

Because of its large size, we used a table saw for cutting the majority of wood for the construction of this cabinet. You may wish to use stock lumber for your cabinet to eliminate some of the rip cuts. For example, the wood for the cleats can be purchased, although we opted to cut our own from the scrap to reduce waste material.

Project note

Predrill and countersink all screw holes to prevent splitting. For ease of construction, use a compressor and nail gun.

Cutting

1 Crosscut each of the twelve 8-foot 1x8 boards to 76½ inches, then rip each to 6½-inch widths for sides and back pieces (A). Trim three of the 12 off-cuts to 18¾ inches, rip each into 1½ inch pieces until there are ten cleats (B).

2 Rip the three 8-foot 1x12 boards to a width of 9 inches for shelves (D). Rip the off-cuts to 1½-inch widths for front and back cleats (C). Crosscut all pieces to 39-inch lengths for a total of six shelves (D) and six front and back cleats (C).

3 From one 8-foot 1x2, cut five 17¼-inch lengths for shelf cleats (E). From the other 8-foot 1x2, cut one more 17¼-inch length for a total of six shelf cleats (E) and one 39-inch length for a total of seven front and back cleats (C).

4 From one 8-foot 1x4 cut one 40½-inch length for top front trim (J) and one 42-inch length for bottom front trim (F).

5 From each of the other two 8-foot 1x4 boards, cut one 69½-inch length and one 19½-inch length for a total of two vertical front trim pieces (I) and two bottom side trim pieces (G).

6 From the 4x4 foot piece of ¾-inch plywood, cut two 18¾x 39-inch pieces for top and bottom (H).

7 From 3½-inch crown molding, cut one 41½-inch short-point to short-point length (K), mitering corners; cut two mirrored pieces of crown molding (L) with one straight end and one mitered end, 19½ inches short-point to square end to match the front miter on each side.

8 Sand all cut edges until smooth; sand flat surfaces as necessary.

Sides

1 For each side panel, lay out three ¾x6½x76½-inch boards (A) on a work surface with edges together and ends flush. Measure and make marks at 2¾ inches, 19½ inches, 35½ inches and 51½ inches from the bottom. Draw reference lines across all three boards at those points. Determine what will be the front of the side panel and mark it.

2 Position five ¾x1½x18¾-inch side cleats (B) across the three side boards, four with the tops of the cleats flush with the drawn lines, and one ¾ inch down from the top edge of the boards with all front edges flush to the front of the assembled side panel. Attach cleats to boards with screws through cleats into boards.

3 Repeat steps 1 and 2 for the remaining side panel. Make sure that the side panels are mirror images of each other, with the cleats facing the inside of the cabinet and flush with the front edges.

Back

1 Assemble the back as you did the sides, using the remaining six ¾x6½x76½-inch boards (A) and five ¾x1½x39-inch back cleats (C). Ends of cleats should be flush with sides of assembled back panel.

Shelves

1 For each shelf, lay out two ¾x9x39-inch boards (D) on a work surface with edges together and ends flush. Measure and make marks 13 inches from each end and draw reference lines across the boards at these marks. Determine which edge will be the front of the shelf and mark it.

OPEN-FRONT TV CABINET
(Actual Sizes)

P	T	W	L	#
A	¾"	6½"	76½"	12
B	¾"	1½"	18¾"	10
C	¾"	1½"	39"	7
D	¾"	9"	39"	6
E	¾"	1½"	17¼"	6
F	¾"	3½"	42"	1
G	¾"	3½"	19½"	2
H	¾"	18¾"	39"	2
I	¾"	3½"	69½"	2
J	¾"	3½"	40½"	1
K	¾"	3½"	41½"	1
L	¾"	3½"	19½"	2

2 Position two ¾x1½x17¼-inch shelf cleats (E) inside the reference lines with front edges flush. Attach with screws through the bottom of the cleats into shelf boards.

3 Repeat steps 1 and 2 for remaining two shelves.

Assemble & finish

1 Butt back panel into side panels and attach with screws through side panels into back cleats (C).

2 Cut arch in bottom front trim piece (F). Mark 4 inches from each end on the bottom edge and 2 inches up from the center bottom of the board. Connect the marks with gentle arcs and cut out with jigsaw. Attach a front cleat (C) to the back side, ¾ inch below the top edge and centered on the board.

3 Attach bottom trim piece (F) to front by nailing into bottom shelf (H).

4 Place plywood bottom shelf (H) on bottom cleats. The top of the shelf should be flush with the top of the bottom trim piece. Secure with screws driven through shelf into cleats.

5 Attach vertical trim pieces (I) to front sides with nails through trim pieces into shelf cleats and cabinet sides.

6 Attach ¾x1½x39-inch cleat (C) to the back of the top trim piece (J) centered side to side and ¾ inch down from the top with screws driven through cleat into trim piece.

7 Attach trim piece (J) to front of cabinet with top and outside edges flush using screws driven through front of trim piece into side cleats (B).

8 Place plywood top (H) on top cleats and attach with screws driven through plywood into cleats.

9 Attach crown molding to front (K) and sides (L) with glue and finish nails, mitering corners.

10 Fill all nail holes with a spackling compound, sand until smooth and remove all dust. For the cabinet shown on page 82, a combination of paint and stain was used. A base coat of latex satin paint was followed by a light sanding in areas to create a distressed look. Finish with a coat of stain followed by a final coat of polyurethane.

11 Place shelves on cleats.

From Shari
This is a very versatile cabinet. You can use it as an entertainment center or in the bedroom to store your favorite jeans and sweaters!

12 Determine the position of the hole on the back of the cabinet for cords. Use a spade bit to drill the hole. To prevent splitting the wood, start the hole on one side, drill halfway through, and then complete the drilling from the opposite side. ∎

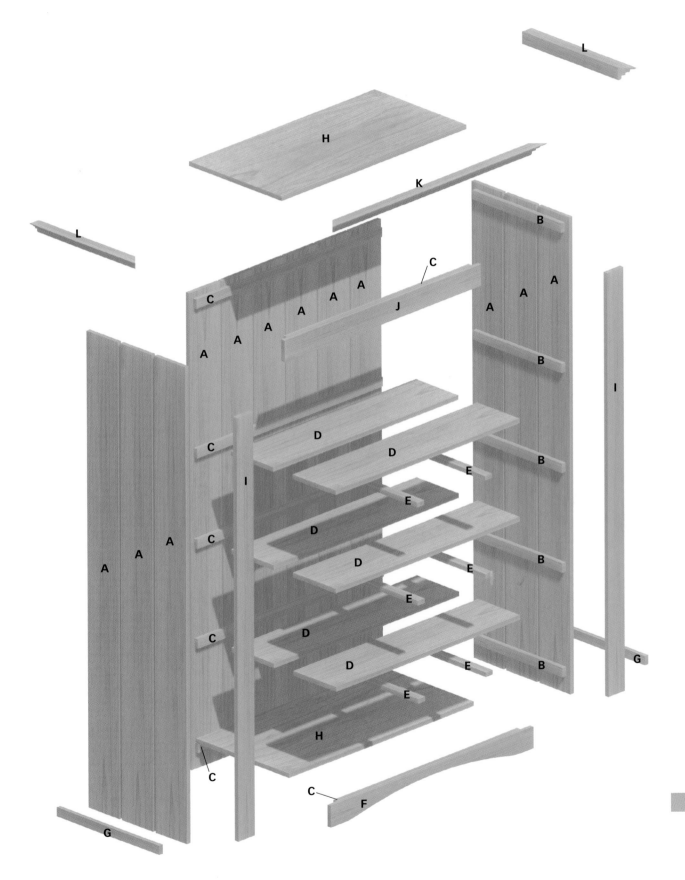

Mirrored Hallway Bench

A tall, mirrored bench with a shelf underneath makes a great place to sit and remove boots or shoes and to hang your coat. The face-height mirror is handy for a quick hair check before you dash out the door.

Project note

This project is made in two pieces—the bench and the mirrored back. The pieces are joined together to create a project that provides both seating and storage.

Back

1 Use a miter saw to cut six 1x2 slats 35¾ inches long (A), two 2x2 stiles 72 inches long (C) (these will be the full height of the project), and three 2x2 cross supports 19½ inches (B) long.

2 Use the router with a ¾-inch straight bit to cut a ¼-inch-deep groove in the center of the length of two of the cross supports (B) for back slats.

3 Using the router with a ¼-inch straight bit, cut a ¼-inch-deep groove in the center of the length of the top support (B) and along the center support (B). These grooves form slots for housing the mirror. The center support (B) should have two grooves, one for the mirror in the top edge and the other groove cut in Step 2 for the slats in the bottom edge.

4 On the top inside edge of each of the stiles (C), rout a 15-inch-long, ¼-inch wide and ¼-inch-deep groove, to support the mirror. Rout this groove from 1½ inches to 16½ inches from the top.

Be sure these grooves line up with the ones cut in the crosspieces.

5 Beginning 1½ inches from each end and working toward the middle, glue the slats into the grooves spacing them 1½ inches apart. Hold in place with 1-inch brads nailed in from the back. Check frequently for squareness and adjust if necessary. Let dry.

6 Using a ⅛-inch drill bit and ⅜-inch countersink bit, drill pilot holes through the sides of the stiles, then join the back slat

If you would like to eliminate routing the grooves for the mirror, cut a piece of ⅛-inch lauan plywood to fit the back opening; nail in place. Cut a piece of mirror to fit opening; glue in place.

TIP

unit to the stiles so the bottom of the bottom cross support is 23¾ inches from the bottom of the stile. Secure with wood glue and 2-inch wood screws into the end of each crosspiece.

7 Predrill for the location of the top crosspiece (B) so the top is ½ inch down from the top of the stile. Slide the mirror down the groove routed into the side stiles until it rests in the groove of the center support. Place the top support (B) in position and secure by repeating step 6.

Seat

1 Cut 1x12 lumber into one 22½-inch top (G), two 13¼-inch sides (F) and one 21-inch bottom (E) to form the seat. Glue and nail

the pieces together by securing the bottom (E) inside of, and flush with, the bottom of the two sides (F), and the top (G) flush with the outside top of the sides; let dry.

2 Cut 1x4 pine into one 24-inch front frame top (H), two 14½-inch front frame sides (I), one 17-inch front frame bottom (J) and four 18-inch side legs (D).

3 Glue and nail two of the side legs (D) flush with the top and front edges of the box side. Glue and nail the other two side legs (D) on the back outside edge flush at the top and with a 1½-inch overhang for attachment to the stiles. Use a leftover piece of stile as a spacer.

4 Glue and nail the top frame piece (H) into the edge of and flush with the seat top and into the box sides. Glue and nail the front frame side pieces (I) into the box side and bottom frame pieces, butting into the bottom of the top piece and flush with the outside of the seat box. Glue and nail the bottom frame piece (J) into the box bottom edge so it begins 2 inches from the bottom of the front frame side pieces.

5 Install the ⅛-inch lauan back (K) by tacking it to the top and bottom box edges.

Finishing

1 Attach the back to the seat with several screws driven into the stile (C) through the back 1x4 legs (D).

2 Fill all nail holes. Glue the wood flush plugs into the large pilot holes. Sand filled holes flush and all rough edges smooth.

3 Prime and paint as desired. For added protection, apply two coats of polyurethane.

4 Add optional coat hooks if desired. ∎

From Matt
For those of you who love tools, a pocket screw could be used instead of drilling pilot holes into the sides of the stiles. This is a very strong joining method—plus it gives you an excuse to purchase a new tool.

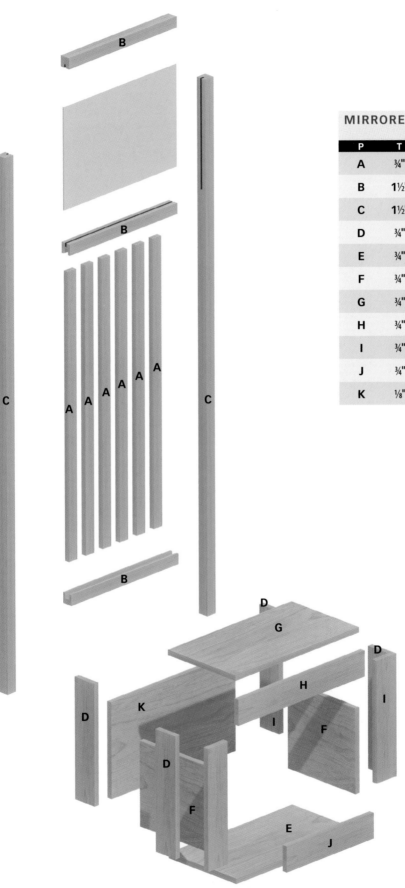

MIRRORED HALLWAY BENCH
(Actual Sizes)

P	T	W	L	#
A	¾"	1½"	35¾"	6
B	1½"	1½"	19½"	3
C	1½"	1½"	72"	2
D	¾"	3½"	18"	4
E	¾"	11¼"	21"	1
F	¾"	11¼"	13¼"	2
G	¾"	11¼"	22½"	1
H	¾"	3½"	24"	1
I	¾"	3½"	14½"	2
J	¾"	3½"	17"	1
K	⅛"	14½"	19½"	1

Train Table

This table features bridges and scenery that will take your child on imaginative road trips and train trips. Hidden plastic storage drawers on rails make putting away toys a snap! Shari's son and I have spent countless hours together designing our dream village.

Project size

49½ inches W x 33¼ inches D x 14½ inches H. **Note:** *This project was constructed to accommodate a purchased scenery board. However, the instructions include how to make one of your own.*

Project note

This project is assembled using a biscuit joiner, biscuits and glue. Follow manufacturer's instructions for marking location of biscuits and cutting slots using biscuit joiner. To make the job go smoother use a compressor and nail gun.

Cutting

1 From each 8-foot oak 1x4, cut one 49½-inch length (for front and back) and one 31¾-inch length (for sides) for table frame.

2 From each 8-foot 1x3, cut six 31¾-inch lengths for tabletop supports.

3 From 1x1 oak, cut six 14½-inch lengths for drawer supports. Rout a ¼x¼-inch rabbet down the center of one side of each drawer support.

4 From 3x3 oak, cut four 11¼-inch lengths for legs.

5 From masonite board, cut one piece 33¼x47¾ inches. Round each corner by tracing the outline of a soup can or round template, then cutting with jigsaw. Sand the curves smooth.

Assemble & finish

1 Glue and nail the drawer supports to the bottoms of the tabletop supports, positioning as shown in Fig. 1 and 2 inches from one end. Make sure you end up with three pairs of tabletop supports, and that the rabbets in their drawer supports are facing each other (see Fig. 1).

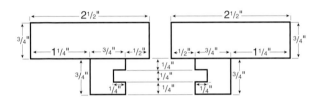

**Fig. 1
One Pair of Drawer Supports
Front View**

2 Referring to Fig. 2, determine the placement of the tabletop supports within the frame. Measure the width of the plastic bins, then subtract 1½ inches. This number is the distance between the edges of the tabletop support pieces when they are joined to the frame. Lay out the tabletop support pieces within the front and back frame pieces and adjust placement as needed to assure adequate clearance for the drawers. Using wood glue and nails, join tabletop supports to front and back table frame pieces with bottom edges flush. Join side table frame pieces to front and back table frame in the same manner.

3 Attach the legs to frame by referring to Fig. 3 for placement. Secure the legs with biscuits and glue.

4 Fill all holes with wood filler. Finish table as desired. ***Note:*** *Using a polyurethane finish, shows the beauty of the wood and is more durable than a painted finish.*

5 Paint tabletop as desired with acrylic paints. Finish with several coats of water-base polyurethane.

6 Insert tabletop into tabletop frame; fill the drawers and set up your child's first train track. Then take a few moments to play with the train set; you may never get this opportunity again! ■

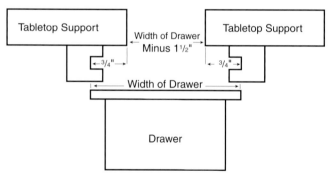

Fig. 2
Drawer Support Placement

From Matt
The drawers here were purchased as a part of a 3-drawer storage cart. We removed the drawers to use for this project!

This project can be assembled without the drawers if desired. Eliminate the drawer supports from the tabletop supports.

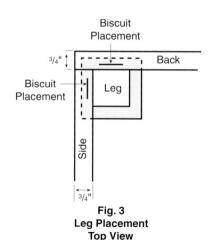

Fig. 3
Leg Placement
Top View

Easy Shelf

Everyone can use more storage shelves, and this unit is exceptionally sturdy and easy to build. If you don't want everyone to see what you've placed on the shelves, sew a cover that attaches to the top of the shelf unit with hook-and-loop tape for easy removal.

Project size

37½ inches W x 11¼ inches D x
83 inches H

Project note

Before purchasing lumber, be sure
the boards are straight and free of
any imperfections.

Cutting

1 Crosscut each 8-foot 1x12 to
83 inches long for sides. If you
use the circular saw to make the
cuts, make sure you use an edge
guide or speed square to ensure
straight cuts.

2 Crosscut the 10-foot 1x12s
to seven 36-inch lengths for
shelves and two 37½-inch lengths
for top and bottom.

3 Crosscut 1x2s to fourteen
11¼-inch lengths for shelf
supports.

Assemble & finish

1 Place side boards side by side
with tops and bottoms even.
Mark sides for the tops of the
shelf supports as desired.

2 Predrill and countersink all
holes for screws. Attach
shelf supports to sides by driving
screws through support into side.

3 Attach top to sides with
screws through top into
sides. Attach bottom to sides with
screws through bottom into sides.

4 Place shelves on shelf
supports. Secure with screws
through shelf into support if
desired.

5 Finish as desired. ∎

From Shari

To add decorator style to your easy shelf, sew two lined fabric panels. Make the height the same as the height of the shelf and the width, wide enough to allow for an overlap at the front. Simply cut two coordinating panels to size, and with right sides facing, sew all the way around leaving an opening to turn the panel right side out. Stitch the opening closed and repeat for the second panel. Overlap the finished panels to fit the shelf and pin. Pin and stitch the loop side of hook-and-loop tape along the top edge, joining the two panels at the same time. Staple the hook side of the tape along three sides of the top edge of the shelf and add the panels. Use a hook-and-loop clasp to hold the panels back and add decorative buttons to the lining side for a nice designer detail.

Wooden Planter Valance

Tired of the traditional gathered fabric valance? Grab your shop tools and create this fabulous wooden one! The added shelf provides a handy place above a window to perch potted silk plants.

Valance

1 Measure the window and determine the valance placement. It must be positioned to cover all blind hardware and still allow for movement. Add an extra 2 inches, plus the thickness of the 1x4 board (¾ inch) for a total of 2¾ inches on each side of the rod or blinds.

2 Cut a 1x4 board to the length determined in Step 1. This valance is for a 72-inch window, so the top length is 77½ inches.

Cut two side pieces each 8 inches long. Attach the side pieces to the bottom of the top piece with wood glue and nails. This frame will be attached above the window and hold the front facing of the valance.

Facing

1 To create the facing of the valance, measure the outside dimension of the frame and cut a length of 1x12 pine lumber 5 inches longer than the frame (82½ inches).

2 Draw and cut out a template for the bottom front of the valance facing. Trace the design onto the 1x12 and cut out with jigsaw using the scroll blade for tight cuts. Sand all edges and remove dust with tack cloth.

Shelf

1 To create the planter shelf, cut a 1x4 board 2 inches shorter than the length of the front facing, or 80½ inches. Determine the placement of the potted plants on the shelf. Cut holes large enough for pots in a 1x4 board by marking the center of each circle and using a compass to draw the diameter needed. Drill a pilot hole on the inside of each circle near the pencil line, and then use a jigsaw to cut out each circle.

2 Mount the planter board as desired to the front face of the valance by using wood glue

From Matt

It is possible to find a hole saw that will cut the size opening needed for the terra-cotta pots. If you're only going to use the hole saw for this project, however, the expense may not be worth the convenience. Use the hole-cutting method outlined in step 1 under Shelf, and save your money to buy silk plants to put in the pots. Real plants won't work well here—the water will just run out of the bottom of the pots onto the floor.

along the edge, securing it from the back with drywall screws. If the valance is long, add additional supports to the planter board.

Finishing

1 Sand all surfaces and remove dust. Prime the frame and valance front. Paint as desired.

2 When completely dry, mount the valance facing/shelf to the frame with the piano hinge (see inset photo page 96). The hinge makes it easier to install

the valance, and also allows the front to flip up, making it easier to remove blinds and clean window.

3 To install the completed valance, use drywall screws to attach the L-brackets to the wall at least 1 inch above the window frame. If the drywall screws do not hit wood, use self anchoring molly bolts to attach the L-brackets. Place the valance in position and attach the frame to the secured L-brackets. ■

Garden Angel

This whimsical angel is the perfect accessory for decorating a flower or vegetable garden. Her wings provide a resting place for small birds, and her cheery face watches over plants in bloom. Exterior paint ensures she'll look great for seasons to come!

SHOPPING LIST

4x4 pressure-treated post:
 one 3-foot length
1x10 pine lumber:
 one 6-foot length
½-inch plywood: 24x24 inches
Baling wire
2-inch galvanized deck screws
Yarn or raffia
Picture-hanging loop
White exterior primer
Exterior paint in desired colors

MATERIALS ON HAND

Circular saw
Jigsaw with scroll blade
Tape measure
Pencil
120-grit sandpaper
Tack cloth
Paintbrushes
Permanent marker

Cutting

1 For base, cut a 7½-inch square of ½-inch plywood and sand smooth with 120-grit sandpaper. Remove dust with tack cloth.

2 Cut a 32-inch length from the 4x4 pressure-treated post for angel body. **Note:** *The circular saw will not be able to cut all the way through the post. Cut halfway through, then flip the post over and cut through from the opposite side.* Sand smooth and remove dust.

3 Attach the 7½-inch plywood square to the bottom of the post using galvanized deck screws. Drill countersink holes for the screws to prevent wobbling.

4 Draw freehand wings on the 6-foot 1x10 board and cut them out with the jigsaw and a scroll blade. The wingspan of the model is approximately 48 inches wide. Sand edges smooth and remove dust.

5 Draw a freehand star and flower on a piece of ½-inch plywood. Cut out the shapes with the jigsaw and a scroll blade. Sand smooth and remove dust.

Assembly & finishing

1 Paint the post and the base with white primer. Use a foam brush and don't worry about great coverage—the rougher the paint job the better. Allow to dry. Select the best side of the post and paint the top 5 inches of that side with a face color. Curve the bottom of the face to form a chin. Paint the remainder of the post with white, then distress the finish by sanding lightly in places.

2 Paint the wings in desired color (model wings are painted with green). Paint the star and flower shapes in desired colors. When all paints are dry, use the permanent marker to draw eyes and a smile. Add a blush to the angel's cheeks with a small amount of pink or red paint applied to a cloth (tap off excess paint until just a tiny amount remains) and rubbed gently on cheek areas of face.

3 Drill countersunk pilot holes in the back of the wings and attach the wings to the post with galvanized deck screws. The top of the wings should be level with the bottom of the chin. Drive a nail into the top of the angel's head and the front of the angel, a few inches under her chin. Drill a hole in the star and run baling wire through it. Wrap wire under star and then wrap wire around the nail in the top of the angel's head. Attach flower using a picture-hanging loop and hang it from the nail on the front of the angel.

4 Cut strands of raffia or yarn for hair. Gather strands into a group and wrap raffia or yarn around center. Nail hair through center to top of post. ∎

> **If your angel is meant to be displayed outside,** make sure you use a primer to paint the base and exterior galvanized screws for assembly. The raffia hair will need to be replaced occasionally.
>
> **TIP**

From Matt

This is by far an all-time favorite project of both Shari's and mine. It's also a great project to use as a fund-raiser—gather together a group of people and make a host of angels. Keep a template of the wings. Draw them on newspaper and cut them out to use again and again.

Also cut out other designs for the front, wreaths for Christmas and pumpkins for Halloween!

Potting Bench

A potting bench is surprisingly easy to build. After you're finished,
you'll wonder how you ever got through gardening chores without one!
You might want to built two and use one as a workbench for your shop.

SHOPPING LIST

1x2: two 8-foot lengths and one 3-foot length

1x4: one 4-foot length, five 6-foot lengths, four 8-foot lengths and one 10-foot length

1x8: one 8-foot length, one 6-foot length and one 10-foot length

¾-inch plywood: one 4x4-foot sheet

1¼-inch galvanized deck screws

Two 12-inch piano hinges

Two wooden knobs

Exterior wood glue

Exterior latex paint

Spar varnish

Paintbrushes

MATERIALS ON HAND

Miter saw

Circular saw with straight-edge or edge guide

Jigsaw

Drill with ⅛-inch bit, #2 driver for screws, and a 2½-inch Forstner bit

Potting Bench Base

Cutting

1 From each of two 6-foot 1x4s, cut two 35¼-inch lengths for a total of four front/back legs (A).

> **If you don't have** or can't find a Forstner bit, a door-hole saw may be used instead. **TIP**

2 Rip two 6-foot 1x4s to 2¾ inches wide. Cut two 35¼-inch lengths from each for a total of four side legs (B).

3 From one 8-foot 1x4, cut two 46½-inch lengths for bottom rails (E). With second 1x4, cut four 21¼-inch lengths for bottom sides and center supports (F) for a total of two E and four F pieces.

4 From the remaining 6-foot 1x4, cut two 24-inch lengths for top side pieces (D).

5 From 10-foot 1x4, cut two 49½-inch lengths for top rails (C).

6 From 8-foot 1x2, cut two 42½-inch lengths for front/back cleats (G).

7 From 3-foot 1x2, cut two 17-inch lengths for side cleats (H).

8 From the 4-foot 1x4, cut one 46½-inch length for back lip (I).

9 From the ¾-inch plywood, cut one 24x48-inch piece for the top shelf (V) and one 22½x46⅝-inch piece for the bottom shelf (W).

Assemble base

Note: Predrill and countersink all screw holes.

1 Referring to Fig. 1, butt side leg (B) into front/back leg (A) and secure with wood glue and three screws along length. Repeat with remaining side legs and front/back legs for a total of four leg units.

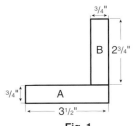

**Fig. 1
Leg Assembly
Top View**

2 Referring to Fig. 2, build the bottom shelf by butting bottom sides and center supports (F) into bottom rails (E) and securing with wood glue and two screws through E into ends of each F.

3 Referring to Fig. 3, butt top sides (D) into top rails (C) and secure with wood glue and two screws through C into ends of each D.

4 Measure 12 inches from the bottom inside of each leg unit and mark. With the leg unit to the outside of each corner, position the bottom of the base shelf assembly at the 12-inch marks and secure each leg with wood glue and screws from the back of the base shelf frame into the leg with 1¼ inch screws.

5 Position the top frame assembly on the outside of the legs so that the top of the assembly is ¾ inch above the top of the legs and secure with wood glue and screws through the back of the leg into the side of the top frame.

6 Attach the front, back and side cleats (G, H) to the inside of the top frame between the legs and with the tops of the cleats

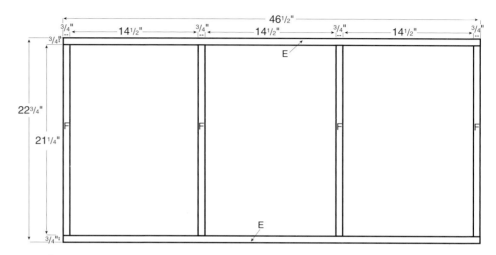

Fig. 2
Bottom Shelf Assembly
Top View

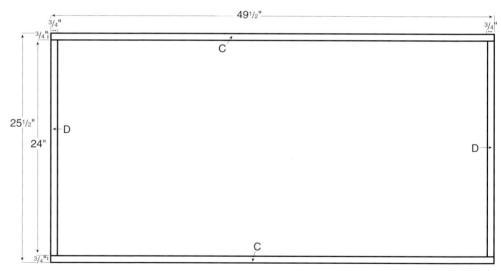

Fig. 3
Top Frame Assembly
Top View

Photo A

Photo B

flush with the tops of the legs (see Photo A).

7 Position the bottom shelf (W) on the bottom shelf support and secure with screws. Position the back lip (I) on top of the bottom shelf between the back

legs and secure with screws (see Photo B).

8 Position the top shelf (V) on the cleats so the top of the plywood is flush with the top of the frame. Secure with screws.

Pickets & Birdhouses
Cutting

1 Cut one 8-foot 1x2 in half for back picket supports (J).

2 From one 8-foot 1x4, cut one 27½-inch length for center picket (K) and two 26½-inch lengths for pickets (L). From another 8-foot 1x4, cut two 24-inch lengths for pickets (M) and two 21½-inch lengths for pickets (N).

3 From one 8-foot 1x8, cut two 28-inch lengths for birdhouse back (O), one 20-inch length for one door (P), two 6-inch lengths for birdhouse top fronts (Q)

and two 2-inch lengths for birdhouse bottom fronts (R).

4 Cut the 6-foot 1x8 in half; from the first half, cut two 8½-inch lengths for long roof sections (S-2). Rip the remainder of the first half to 6½ inches wide, then cut two 8½-inch lengths for short roof sections (S-1). Rip the second half to 5¾ inches wide, then cut into four 5¾-inch lengths for shelves (T).

5 From 10-foot 1x8, cut one 20-inch length for another door (P). Rip the remainder to 5¾ inches wide. Cut four 24½-inch lengths for sides (U).

Note: *Refer to Fig. 4 for steps 6–8.*

6 Find the center of the top of the birdhouse top front pieces (Q) and mark (approximately 3⅝ inches from each side). Measure and mark 2½ inches from the bottom corners and connect these points with the top center point by drawing a line. Cut on the lines to form the birdhouse peak.

7 Using the Forstner bit, cut a 2½-inch hole centered in the piece.

8 Find the center of the birdhouse back pieces (O) and mark approximately 3⅝ inches from each side. Measure and mark 3½ inches from the top corners and connect these points with the top center point by drawing a line. Cut on the lines to form the birdhouse peak.

Note: *Refer to Fig. 5 for step 9.*

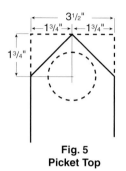

Fig. 5
Picket Top

9 Find center of each picket (K, L, M and N) and mark approximately 1¾ inch from top. Measure down 1¾ inch on each side and mark. Draw lines to connect the points and trim off points with jigsaw.

10 Using Forstner bit, drill a 2½-inch-diameter hole, centered on a point 1¾ inches from the top and sides of the picket.

Assemble birdhouses

Note: *Be aware of which side of the potting table the birdhouse will be attached, and make sure the birdhouses are mirror images of each other.*

1 Butt sides (U) into birdhouse back (O) with bottoms flush and secure with wood glue and two screws through back into sides.

2 Butt bottom front (R) against sides (U) with bottoms flush and secure with wood glue and screws through front into sides.

3 Position the shelves (T) inside the birdhouse and secure with wood glue and screws through the sides and back.

4 Attach piano hinges to doors (P), then attach hinges to birdhouse sides (U), allowing a slight space between the door and the bottom front so the door swings freely. **Note:** *Hinges should be located on the outer sides of the two birdhouses, so the doors open from the center to the outside. Attach knobs to doors.*

5 Attach top front pieces (Q) to sides (U), again allowing a slight space between the door and top front so the door swings freely.

6 Attach the short roof sections (S-1) (the right section for the left birdhouse, and the left section for the right birdhouse) with wood glue and screws through the roof into the front and back (see Fig. 6). Attach the long sections of roof (S-2) on the opposite sides.

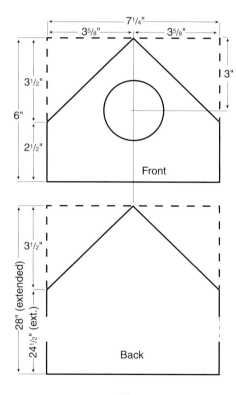

Fig. 4
Birdhouse
Front & Back Peaks

Assemble picket section

1 Locate and mark center of back picket supports (J) and 7 inches from each end.

2 Place center picket (K) face-down on work surface. Place next two pickets (L) on each side of K, approximately 1¼ inches away. Lay out remaining pickets (M and N), using back picket support (J) as a straightedge to line up the bottoms of the pickets. **Note:** *Pickets should not go past the 7-inch mark at each end of the back picket support (J). If they do, readjust the spacing between them until all pickets fall within this space.*

3 Lay one back picket support (J) over the pickets arranged on the work surface, approximately 6 inches from the bottom of the pickets. Make sure the centers of back picket support (J) and picket K are lined up. Secure back picket support (J) to pickets with wood glue and screws driven through support into pickets. Position the other back picket support (J) approximately 6 inches from the top of center picket (K) and secure with wood glue and screws through back picket support (J) into pickets.

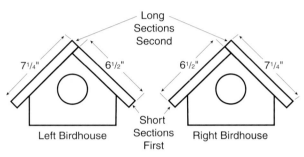

Long Sections Second

7¼" 6½" 6½" 7¼"

Left Birdhouse

Short Sections First

Right Birdhouse

Fig. 6 Roof

From Matt

If you decide you want the birdhouse and the top picket to be removable, do not attach the birdhouse to the table. Assemble the pickets to the houses, but use mending plates to attach the entire assembly to the table. Use two plates, one for each birdhouse, and attach to the bench with screws. When you want to remove the birdhouses and pickets for storage, simply un-screw the plates and remove.

Final assembly

1 Position the birdhouses at the rear corners of the potting bench with back and side edges flush. Lightly mark the outlines of the birdhouses in pencil on the potting-bench top. Predrill several pilot holes through the bottom of the bench top inside the pencil lines.

2 Run a thin bead of glue around the bottom edges of the birdhouses and reposition on the bench top. Attach with screws through the predrilled pilot holes. Remove excess glue if necessary.

3 Set the picket section in place on the bench top between the birdhouses and mark the location of the back picket supports on the backs of the birdhouses. Predrill several pilot holes through the back picket supports into the birdhouse backs. Apply glue to the bottoms of the pickets and secure back picket supports to the birdhouse backs. Remove excess glue if necessary.

Finish

1 Paint as desired using an exterior latex paint if the bench will be used outside.

2 Apply spar varnish for extra years of durability. ■

P	T	W	L	#
POTTING BENCH (Actual Sizes)				
A	¾"	3½"	35¼"	4
B	¾"	2¾"	35¼"	4
C	¾"	3½"	49½"	2
D	¾"	3½"	24"	2
E	¾"	3½"	46½"	2
F	¾"	3½"	21¼"	4
G	¾"	1½"	42½"	2
H	¾"	1½"	17"	2
I	¾"	3½"	46½"	1
J	¾"	1½"	47⅞"	2
K	¾"	3½"	27½"	1
L	¾"	3½"	26½"	2
M	¾"	3½"	24"	2
N	¾"	3½"	21½"	2
O	¾"	7¼"	28"	2
P	¾"	7¼"	20"	2
Q	¾"	7¼"	6"	2
R	¾"	7¼"	2"	2
S-1	¾"	6½"	8½"	2
S-2	¾"	7¼"	8½"	2
T	¾"	5¾"	5¾"	4
U	¾"	5¾"	24½"	4
V	¾"	24"	48"	1
W	¾"	22½"	46⅝"	1

From Shari
This potting bench won't attract just gardeners, don't be surprised if your winged and footed friends make use of it as well!

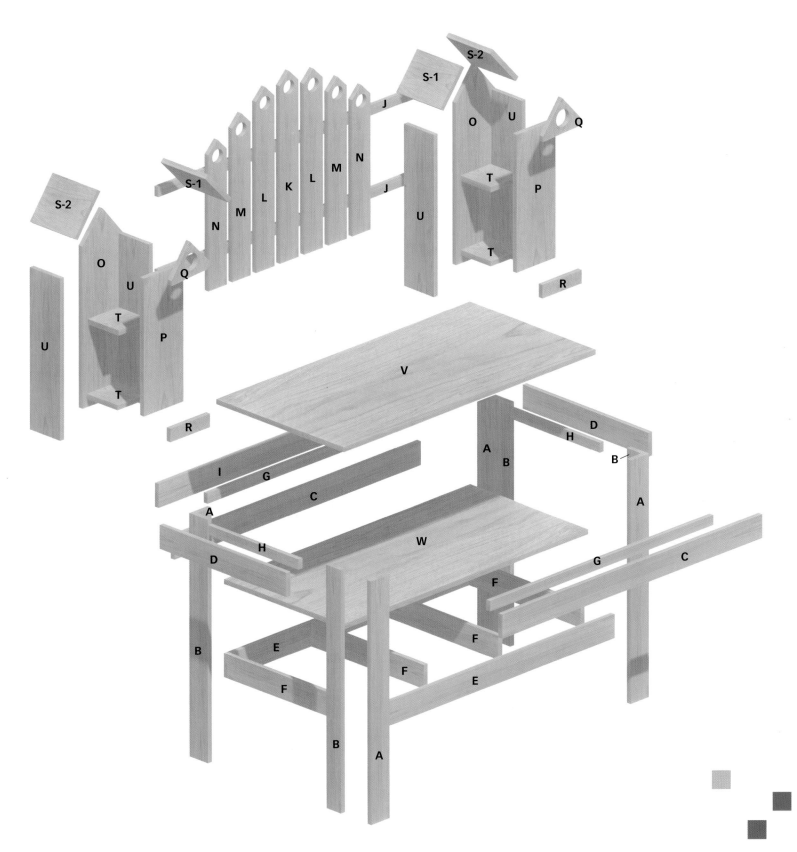

Oak Toy Shelf

Keeping their toys picked up will be a snap when your kids have a shelf of their own. Sized just right for baskets and books, this shelf may be painted or stained to match their rooms or your family-room decor.

Project size

59½ inches W x 14½ inches D x 43½ inches H

Project note

A biscuit joiner can be used for the process of constructing the shelf panels, which will make a stronger joint than just gluing the two boards together. Remember to remove the excess glue immediately with a damp sponge.

Ends

1 Cut each 8-foot 1x8 into two 48-inch lengths. Glue up and clamp two sets of two 48-inch lengths with one end flush for a total of two 14½ x 48-inch panels for ends. Let dry. Remove glue drips, and sand or plane smooth.

2 Crosscut each end (C) to 43½ inches. Transfer handle and bottom detail patterns to top and bottom of each end. Drill an access hole for the jigsaw blade, and cut out handle and bottom detail (page 111). ***Tip:*** *Clamp the two sides together before making the cut. This will ensure that the handle and bottom details match exactly.*

3 Round over the top and side edges of each end. Do not round over the handle cutout or bottom detail.

Shelves

1 Cut each 10-foot 1x8 into two 60-inch lengths. Glue up and clamp three sets of two 60-inch lengths with one end flush for a total of three 14½x60-inch panels for shelves. Let dry. Remove glue drips and sand or plane smooth.

2 Rip each shelf to 13¼ inches wide. Crosscut each shelf (A) to 58 inches.

3 Referring to Fig. 1, round over three edges of the 10-foot 1x2s. Cut a ⅜x¾-inch rabbet in the remaining edge. Crosscut each 10-foot length into two 58-inch lengths for shelf trim pieces (B). Sand smooth. ***Note:*** *For ease of construction, attach the 1x2 directly to the shelf with wood glue and nails.*

Assemble & finish

1 Glue and clamp shelf trim panels to shelves and let dry (Fig. 2).

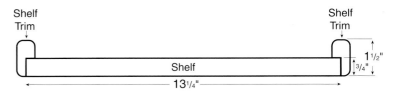

**Fig. 1
Shelf Trim Profile**

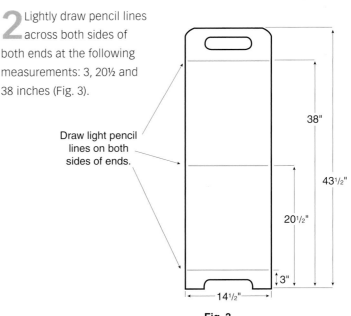

**Fig. 2
Shelf Assembly End View**

2 Lightly draw pencil lines across both sides of both ends at the following measurements: 3, 20½ and 38 inches (Fig. 3).

Draw light pencil lines on both sides of ends.

**Fig. 3
Shelf Placement**

3 Align bottom of bottom shelf with the lines at the 3-inch mark and drill three or four pilot holes with countersinks through each end into the end of the shelf. Attach shelf with countersunk screws and glue in plugs, matching grain.

4 Attach remaining shelves in the same manner, matching bottoms of shelves with 20½- and 38-inch lines. Trim plugs with flush-cut saw.

5 Stain and finish as desired (water-based polyurethane is recommended for items to be used by children). ∎

From Matt

If you decide not to use the plugs, stain the piece first, and then match the wood putty to the stain. Most stain manufacturers also carry a matching wood putty shade. After the stain has dried, apply the putty and wipe flush to the surface with a clean cloth.

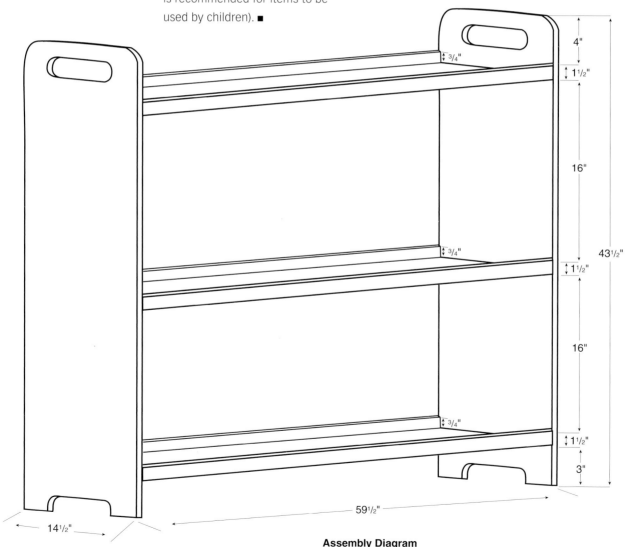

Assembly Diagram

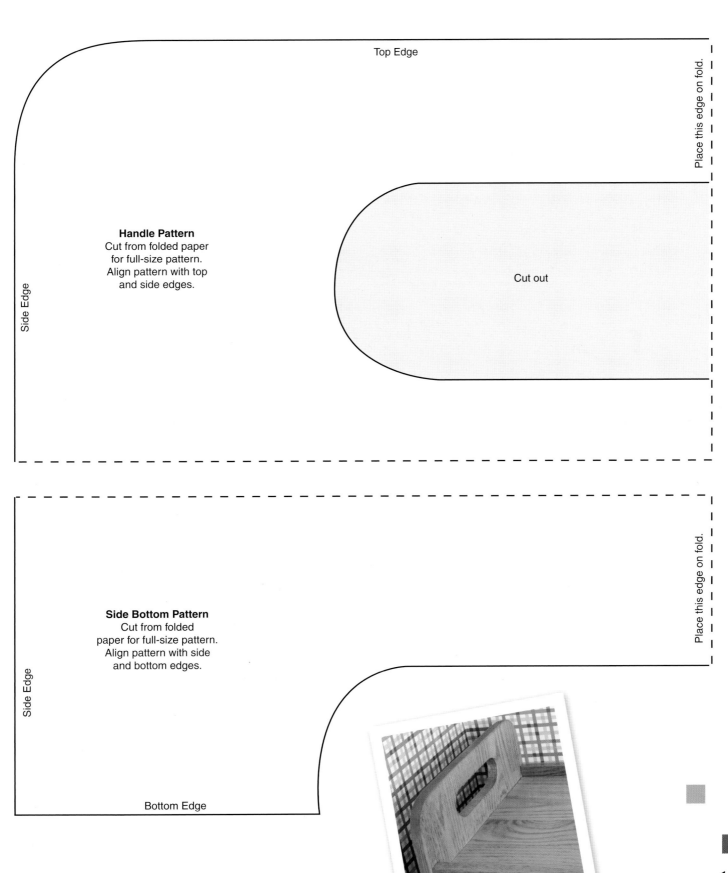

Top Edge

Place this edge on fold.

Handle Pattern
Cut from folded paper
for full-size pattern.
Align pattern with top
and side edges.

Cut out

Side Edge

Place this edge on fold.

Side Bottom Pattern
Cut from folded
paper for full-size pattern.
Align pattern with side
and bottom edges.

Side Edge

Bottom Edge

OAK TOY SHELF (Actual Sizes)				
P	**T**	**W**	**L**	**#**
A	¾"	13¼"	58"	3
B	¾"	1½"	58"	6
C	¾"	14½"	43½"	2

Pot & Pan Rack

A hanging pot and pan rack is perfect for larger kitchens with high ceilings. Hanging cooking pots and cooking utensils also frees up cabinet space for other storage.

Project size

51½ inches W x 31 inches D x 11¼ inches H

Frame

1 Cut two pieces of 1x12 lumber, each 50 inches long (A), and two pieces 28 inches long (B). Butt the 28-inch pieces (B) into the 50-inch pieces (A) and assemble into a frame using wood glue and a nail gun.

Cleats

1 Using 1x4 lumber, cut two 48½-inch long cleats (C) and two 21-inch short cleats (D).

2 Attach long cleats (C) to the inside top edges of the box sides for hanging. Drill pilot holes through the outside of the frame into the edge of the cleat and secure with glue and drywall screws.

3 Attach the short cleats (D) between the long cleats securing through the short frame sides.

Trim

1 Use the miter saw to cut decorative molding to length using 45-degree angles for pieces E and F. Place the decorative trim around the top and bottom of the frame and install with wood glue and the nail gun.

Finishing

1 Sand the entire box; remove dust with a tack cloth. Paint inside and outside of box and trim as desired. When dry, paint all surfaces with two coats of satin-finish water-base polyurethane.

2 Mark position of hooks. Drill pilot holes in bottom edge and screw hooks in position.

3 Decide where to place the frame on the ceiling. Locate the ceiling joists and mark the corresponding location on the cleats. Drill a pilot hole through the cleat at each mark. Place frame in position and secure to the ceiling using molly bolts through the cleats. Firmly tighten. ∎

From Matt

The toughest challenge of this project is hanging it. You'll need to recruit a partner (pizza makes a great bribe). One of you will need to hold the frame in position while the other does the attaching. If you are lucky, you'll have a ceiling joist in the right spot for attaching at least one side or end of the pot rack.

If the center of the room isn't a convenient place to hang a rack for pots and utensils, consider hanging them as a functional window topper. Just choose a metal drapery rod in an appropriate weight and add a few S-hooks to hang most pans and utensils in style. Or, add a board with S-shaped hangers along the wall edge of the soffit as shown in the photo above.

POT & PAN RACK
(Actual Sizes)

P	T	W	L	#
A	¾"	11¼"	50"	2
B	¾"	11¼"	28"	2
C	¾"	3½"	48½"	2
D	¾"	3½"	21"	4
E	¾"	1½"	51½"	4
F	¾"	1½"	31"	4

TIP

Here's something to consider, we took this opportunity to eliminate the fluorescent ceiling fixture above the kitchen island and replace it with a rectangle of track and six halogen lights. Now the island glows with a warmth that wasn't possible with the fluorescent fixture. The entire room benefits from the reflected light off the countertop.

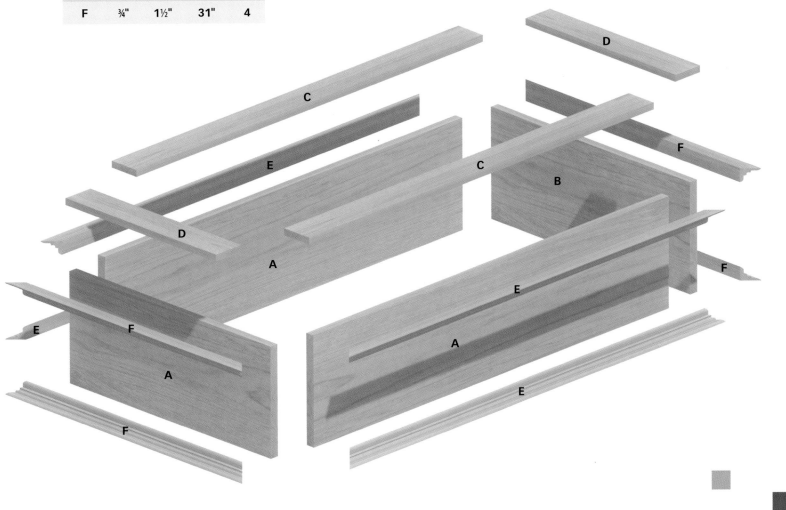

Breakfast Bed Tray

This tray is perfect for serving breakfast in bed on those special occasions, or as a terrific decorative display tray that can be placed on an oversized ottoman or table. Decorate it for any season and it will be a treasured project for years to come.

Project size

28 inches W x 18 inches D x
4 inches H

Project notes

Instead of using plywood with its unsightly edge, purchase pine panels to allow you to construct larger wood projects without gluing several boards together to get wider widths. Depending on the size you desire, panels can be purchased from 16 to 32 inches wide and from 24 to 72 inches long. You can find them in most home-center stores.

The decorative posts are used for enhancing moldings such as crown molding and fascias.

Steps

1 Crosscut the panel to 18x28 inches using a circular saw and an edge guide. Remember when cutting with a circular saw to cut with the best side of the wood facing down.

2 With a miter saw, cut two end pieces 14½ inches long, and two side pieces 24 inches long from 1x3 poplar board. Sand the pieces smooth using the 120-grit sandpaper.

3 Using the miter saw, cut the four decorative corner posts so that the post is about ½ inch higher than the 1x3 piece of poplar.

4 Rout the edge of the tray panel using the router with a roman ogee bit with a bearing (the bearing follows the outer edge of the panel, allowing a nice smooth routed edge). Sand the edges smooth.

5 Using a carpenter's square or tape measure, locate the layout of the 1x3 pieces and the corner posts on the tray panel. The 1x3s should be in from the edges of the panel approximately 1 inch around the perimeter. The four decorative posts should be placed at all four corners. Draw a pencil line around the outer edge of the boards for reference.

6 Glue all the pieces using wood glue, place into position and clamp. Remove any excess glue immediately with a damp cloth. If the glue is not removed it will not take the stain and will look patchy. Clamp all the pieces into position and allow to dry overnight.

7 Sand all the edges smooth and remove dust with a soft cloth. Stain the tray with desired wood stain color. Allow to dry and apply wipe-on polyurethane. Several coats may be desired, just follow manufacturer's suggestions for dry time and prep between coats. ∎

From Matt
This simple tray took me about 1 hour to complete, using things that are already available. That is my little trick to woodworking. I may not have all the tools to turn or rout decorative molding, but someone has already done it for me. Check out all the areas of your local home center for unique building supplies that can be modified for any project.

Fireplace Mantel

A roaring fire can help tame the fiercest winter weather, but not all fireplaces are created equally in a decorating sense. Without a mantel it seems somehow incomplete. Fortunately, adding a mantel is one decorating problem that is easily solved!

1x4, 1x8 and 1x6 poplar lumber

Finish nails

1¼-inch drywall screws

Wood screws

Square drawer pulls

Caulk

Double-stick tape

Wood glue

Spackle compound

Desired paint or stain

Primer appropriate for desired paint or stain

Small wooden buttons

Dowel screws for drawer pulls

MATERIALS ON HAND

Circular saw

Jigsaw with scroll blade

Miter saw

Router table and router with chamfer bit

Drill

Level

Scrap paper

Pencil

150- and 220-grit sandpaper

Tack cloth

Paintbrushes

Project notes

This project is basically a shelf unit that is attached to a flat-front fireplace. In this situation, the facing of the fireplace was a paneled wall above the hearth. If the facing of your fireplace is brick or stone, you may need masonry tools to install the mantel.

Steps

1 Using circular saw, cut a 1x8 to the length of the hearth opening; cut a 1x6 piece 2 inches longer than the length of the 1x8. These two boards will be joined to create an L-shaped shelf with the 1x8 attached to the fireplace as a back support, and the 1x6 creating the long shelf.

2 Before attaching the two boards, use a router table and a chamfer bit to bevel a ¼-inch detail along the edges and sides of each piece, excluding the edge of the two boards where they will be attached.

3 Connect the two pieces at a 90-degree angle with wood glue and finish nails.

Secure the shelf unit to the fire-place using drywall screws spaced evenly across the board (see photo on page 118). *Note: If the fireplace is surrounded with stone or masonry, use the correct fastener for the type of surface. Place the screws at the location of the small curved supports detailed in the next step. The supports will hide the screws. Don't forget to use a level for this step. All other screws were covered with small wooden buttons.*

4 Cut and attach small curved supports where the pieces meet to add extra strength to the top shelf. To make the supports, first sketch the desired design on a piece of scrap paper to use as a template. Tape two 1x4 boards together with double-stick tape so that they can be cut at the same time. Trace the template design on the 1x4 boards and cut out using the jigsaw with a scroll blade. *Note: Cut as close as possible to the pencil lines. Sand the pieces smooth using the pencil lines as a guide. Separate the boards and remove the tape.*

5 Use the router table and chamfer bit to make angled trim molding by running a 1x4 through the table. Only one edge of the 1x4 needs to be routed.

6 Cut the 1x4 trim material to length using a miter saw, using 45-degree cuts at the corners where the front and side pieces meet. Attach the trim using wood glue and small finish nails to the outer edge of the top shelf (see photo on this page). Fill all nail holes using spackle compound. Sand smooth and remove all dust.

7 For more interest, add square drawer pulls along the 1x8 back support, using dowel screws to attach them.

8 Caulk around the edges. Prime and paint mantel as desired. ∎

From Matt

If you don't have a fireplace, this project makes a terrific shelf. Just follow the same steps, but attach the unit to a wall instead of a fireplace.

TIP **As much as we would all like to own a router table,** sometimes all we can afford is the router. No problem—you can still complete this project. Just purchase router bits with roller bearings as part of the bit. This type of bit is used as a guide to make router cuts on lengths of boards. Router guides can also be purchased to install on your router, which will ensure straight cuts.

SEWING PROJECTS

Even if you don't know how to sew,
or don't have a sewing machine,
there are projects here for you.
Did you know that window coverings
can be made without sewing a stitch?

Ruffled Bed Skirt

A bed skirt can be ruffled or tailored, depending on the style of the bedroom. Also referred to as duster, dust ruffle or bed valance, bed skirts serve to finish off the bed so that the springs and underside are not visible. Of course Matt says they exist to hide everything that you kick under the bed!

Project note

Some bed skirts have an elastic edge around the ruffle to hold them in place on top of the box spring, but these tend to slip and slide. Attaching the ruffle to a flat piece of fabric that fits on top of the box spring under the mattress provides a secure anchor for the ruffle and helps hold it in place.

Steps

1 To be sure that the flat section that makes up the top of the bed skirt will not be seen from the side, it needs to be cut slightly smaller than the top of the box spring. Measure the length of the box spring and add 1⅝ inches for the hem and seam allowance. Measure the width of the box spring and add 1¼ inches for the seam allowance. Cut the top of the bed skirt to these measurements, piecing fabric if necessary.

2 To determine the height of the bed skirt, measure the distance from the top of the box springs to the floor and add 2⅝ inches for the seam allowance and hem.

3 For beds with footboards the bed skirt should have two sides and a separate end piece. To determine the amount of fabric needed for each side, measure the length of the box springs and multiply by 2½ to allow for gathering. Divide this number by the width of fabric (54 inches, for example) and round up to the next whole number. Multiply this number by the height of the bed skirt determined in step 2.

4 To determine the amount of fabric for the end piece, measure the width of the box springs and multiply by 2½. Divide this number by the width of the fabric and round up to the next whole number. Multiply this number by the height of the bed skirt determined in step 2.

Note: *To accommodate beds without footboards, determine the total length of the bed skirt (multiply the length of the box springs times two and add the width of the box springs) and multiply this number times 2½ to allow for gathering.*

To determine the amount of fabric needed, divide the number obtained above by the width of the fabric (54 inches, for example) and round up to the nearest whole number. Multiply this number by the height of the bed skirt determined in step 2.

5 For a professional look, patterns in printed fabric should be matched. To determine the pattern match: Lay the fabric right side up on the work surface. Mark the top of the first complete pattern repeat in the fabric with a pin.

Measure from the top of the pattern to the end of the repeat. This measurement should be divided into the measurement achieved in step 3. Round up to the next whole number and then this is the cutting length for each piece of fabric.

6 Stitch the pieces together. If the bed does not have a footboard, the ruffle should be stitched together in one continuous piece. If the bed does have a footboard, sew two sides and a bottom piece.

7 When ruffle is complete, fold under the short-side ends ½ inch twice and sew. Fold up the bottom edge 1 inch twice for hem and sew.

8 Gather the ruffle to fit the flat top piece. The easiest way to gather such large pieces of fabric is to zigzag-stitch a piece of strong string or thin cord along the raw top edge of the piece (being careful to not catch the string or cord in the stitching). Anchor the string at one end with a pin and gently pull on the other end, adjusting the gathers as you go.

9 Attach one side of the bed skirt, or the entire skirt to the top with right sides facing. Pin in place, making sure the gathers are evenly spaced. Machine-stitch the skirt to the top using a ⅝-inch seam allowance. To strengthen the seam and give a neater appearance, zigzag a second seam next to the first straight seam and trim the excess fabric. Repeat for the second side and the bottom piece if needed.

10 Place the bed skirt on the box spring, and smooth the sides and bottom into position. Place the mattress over the box spring and make the bed. ■

From Shari

For one of my bed-skirt projects, I used an old bed skirt as the base for my new one and just sewed the new skirting over the top of the old one. This gave the new skirt more weight and a richer appearance. At the same time, I didn't waste the old dust ruffle.

Duvet Cover

A bedroom should offer more
than just a place to sleep after a long day—
it should be a retreat, a place to let daytime worries fade away. One way
to create a warm and inviting sanctuary is through the use of fabrics
that make you feel good. A duvet cover that utilizes your favorite fabrics
can produce a comforting retreat from even your most hectic days.

Project note

Our duvet cover was made out of three coordinating fabrics. The large floral was the front fabric, a smaller-scale stripe was the backing, and a tiny check was used for the piping and to cover the buttons. Since we were making a queen-sized duvet, both the top and the backing had to be pieced with a center panel and a second panel split and attached to each side to give us enough width.

Steps

1 Measure the duvet to be covered to determine the length and width of the cover. Add 3¾ inches to the width (1¼ inch for twin sizes). For the length, calculate the front and the backing separately. For the backing, add 1¼ inch to the length for seam allowances. For the front, add 5½ inches to the length for seam allowances and the button and buttonhole facing.

2 To determine how many lengths of fabric you will need, divide the width of the duvet by the width of the fabric you are using and round up to a whole number. For example, if your duvet is 80 inches wide and the fabric is 54 inches wide, add 3¾ inches to the width, making the total width 83¾ inches. Next, divide 83¾ by 54 for approximately 1.5. Round this up to the nearest whole number, which is 2. You will need 2 lengths of fabric for the top and 2 lengths for the backing.

Next, multiply the number of lengths by the actual length needed. For example, if the duvet is 90 inches long, add 5½ inches for the top, making the total length 95½ inches. Multiply 95½ times 2 lengths for a total of 191 inches, or 5⅓ yards. Consider you will need this same amount

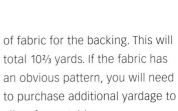

of fabric for the backing. This will total 10⅔ yards. If the fabric has an obvious pattern, you will need to purchase additional yardage to allow for matching.

3 Begin by cutting the 4 lengths of fabric required to the appropriate length. Cut one panel of the top and one of the backing in half lengthwise to split and attach to the sides of the matching panel to get the proper width required. Once the half panels are sewn to the full panel, cut off any excess to bring the

top and backing to the appropriate cut widths as figured in step 1. Sew the side sections to the center section to form the full-size top and bottom pieces of the duvet cover.

4 Determine the position of the button opening on the duvet. It can be anywhere from just below the position of the pillows to halfway down the duvet. Cut the top across the width at this location. Do not cut the backing. Hem the cut edge of the bottom half by turning the edge over

To make this project go a little quicker, purchase ready-made piping in a coordinating color or try eliminating the piping all together. Instead of covering your own buttons, use store-bought ones that can be just as pretty!

TIP

½ inch then 2 inches. This will give the fabric support for adding the buttons. Cut 3 inches off of the edge of the top half. This will become the facing for the buttonholes (see photo on page 125). Hem one edge of the facing by turning the fabric over ¼ inch twice; stitch.

5 One method for making the custom-covered piping is to lay the fabric flat, wrong side up and folding one corner to the opposite selvage edge, lining the cut edge of the fabric up against the selvage edge to create a triangle. Press fold in place, open the fabric and with a straight-edge, follow the fold line to draw out bias strips at a width of three times the circumference of the cord plus 1 inch. Sew the strips together and press the seam open. Fold the strip in half and wrap it around the cord right side to the outside. Use the zipper foot on your machine and stitch close to the cord.

6 Sew the cord and the facing along the edge of the top half of the duvet, and then mark and sew buttonholes where desired.

7 Sew cord all the way around the outside edge of the bottom piece. Overlap the top pieces, pin in place to hold, and place right sides together with the backing. Pin in place and sew outside seams. Trim the seam allowance if needed and clip any excess at the corners; turn the duvet cover right side out.

8 Cover buttons following manufacturer's instructions. Sew buttons in place to match buttonholes. ■

From Shari

Notice in the photo that we even used a fourth fabric for the dust ruffle and in some of the accessory pillows. The combination came together easily since the fabrics were coordinated for us at the fabric store. This can make pattern mixing a piece of cake!

Quilted Valance

A quilted valance is a nice way to add depth and richness to window treatments without building a padded cornice board. Choose the fabric carefully so that the quilting is effective and achievable.

Project note

If you are mounting this quilted valance over draperies, you may need to use 1x6 boards for framework construction instead of 1x4 boards, to give the draperies enough clearance.

Steps

1 Determine the location of the three-sided framework to hold the quilted valance. Generally, the framework is mounted 4 inches above any existing window treatment and a few inches to either side to leave room for the existing treatment to move. The side piece should measure 1 inch shorter than the actual length of the finished valance. Take measurements and jot them down on scrap paper.

2 Build the framework. Cut the top piece and the two side pieces to length using a miter saw or handsaw. Attach the sides to the underside of the top piece by drilling small pilot holes through the top and side, and then attaching with wood screws.

3 When the three-sided framework is built, wrap it in the lining fabric and attach with staples.

4 Install the framework over the window using L-brackets attached to the wall with self-anchoring molly bolts. Make sure the framework is level. ***Note:*** *The finished framework will help you measure for the valance.*

5 Measure the width (including around the side pieces to the wall) and the height (measuring just from the front of the framework and extending down below the side pieces at least 1 inch). A second piece that will not get quilted is required to complete the valance and it is the size of the top frame board plus ⅝-inch seam allowance all the way around. Before cutting, add 3 inches to the height and 6 inches to width of the larger piece to allow for shrinkage from quilting.

6 Cut out the valance panels. Cut a lining panel and quilt batting to match both. For longer windows, the valance and lining fabrics may need to be pieced.

7 Layer the lining fabric (right side down), the quilt batting, and the front valance fabric (right side up). Pin together, from the center out, approximately 4–6 inches apart.

8 Start the quilting process with the tension on the machine loosened a bit. You may want to practice the technique on a sandwich of scrap fabrics and batting before stitching on the valance fabric. Make the stitched outlines very general and sweeping, and avoid tight detailing that can bunch up the fabric and take up a lot of time. When the quilting is complete, remove the pins.

9 Remeasure the valance to the specific measurements taken for the finished valance in step 5. Add 1¼ inches to the height and 2 inches to the length and trim to size. If you are making a soft scallop at the bottom, cut it at this time.

10 Cut another piece of lining fabric to match the quilted valance piece, including any scallops at the bottom. Cut two pieces of cord to match the width of the valance at the top and the width at the bottom, following the line of the scallop.

11 Pin the cord to the front face of the valance at the top straight edge and the scalloped edge. Make sure that the cord stops 1 inch short of each end by pulling the cord into the valance at that point so as not to leave any raw edges.

12 Center and pin the strip of valance fabric along the top edge of the trim and valance, and machine-stitch in place using the zipper foot.

13 Center and pin the lining strip to the top edge of the extra lining piece cut in step 10 and stitch in place. Press seam open.

14 Pin the lining piece to the valance and trim piece with right sides facing. Stitch all the way around leaving a wide opening unsewn along the very top edge. Remove the pins, trim the seam allowances, clip the curves and turn the valance right side out. Hand-stitch the opening closed.

15 Pin the soft side of the hook-and-loop tape to the inside edge of the valance along the edges that will touch the wall, and machine-stitch in place.

16 Fold the top edge down so the ends meet with the top edges of the sides of the valance. Hand-stitch the edges together to create a corner.

17 Staple the hook side of the hook-and-loop tape to the edge of the top and side boards of the framework, next to the wall.

18 Position the valance on the framework, centering it and smoothing it with your hands. Fold the sides around to meet the wall. ∎

From Shari

This valance could have been made more easily if it didn't have a top piece to it. Simply position the hook portion of the hook-and-loop tape on the front edge of the top framework piece including around the corner to the wall. Add a piece on the side board just as we described above. Then, the valance is a simple rectangle and much less complicated.

Pillow Shams

Pillow shams are a great way to add more pillows to your bed! I always tell Matt that they are needed for adding height to the bedding, as well as a mix of patterns and textures—giving the entire ensemble a more interesting look. They are fairly easy to make, and in the process, you'll save some money; that's usually when he agrees.

Project note

These instructions are for 24-inch-square Euro pillow forms. Alter the measurements to fit your pillow form.

Steps

1 Begin by measuring the width and height of the pillow form. Determine the appropriate size flange for your pillow. The flange on the model shown is 2½ inches. Cut the front fabric and the craft felt to the width of the pillow plus 5 inches for flange and 1¼ inches for seams. Cut the height the same height as the pillow plus 5 inches for flange and 1¼ inches for seams.

2 The back of the sham is in two pieces that overlap so that the pillow form can be inserted and removed. To determine the size of the two fabric pieces, measure the width of the pillow form, add 5 inches for flange, 1¼ inches for seams and an additional 7 inches for overlap and finishing raw edges. For the height, the back pieces should measure the same height as the front piece.

3 Prepare the front by machine-basting the felt to the wrong side of the front pillow sham fabric within the ⅝-inch seam allowance.

4 Prepare the back pieces by folding the overlap edge over ½ inch twice and sewing in place.

5 With right sides facing, line up the back pieces with the front, overlapping the back pieces to match the width of the front piece. Pin fabric pieces together and machine-stitch all the way around the outside edge.

6 Clip corners and cut away some of the felt at the seam allowances to reduce the thickness. Turn the sham right side out and press seams.

7 Pin through all layers to create the flange 2½ inches in from the sewn edge. Using a fabric measuring tape, measure to keep track of the 2½-inch width, slowly topstitch the flange in all the way around the pillow sham.

8 Insert the pillow form into the sham and go dress that bed! ∎

If the front fabric for the pillow sham is a sturdy weight, you will not need to add the craft felt for stiffness. It is there to help hold the flange upright.

TIP

From Shari

If you are making two pillow shams using printed fabrics, make sure to cut the exact match for both pillow sham fronts for a more professional, finished appearance.

Projects sewing Projects Sewing Pro
Projects sewing projects Sewing Projects
Projects sewing projects Sewing Projects Projects
Projects projects Sewing Projects Projects

No-Sew Pull-Back Drapes

Pull-back draperies add a touch of elegance to any room, and they frame windows beautifully. This project gives even non-sewers the ability to have custom-created draperies throughout their homes.

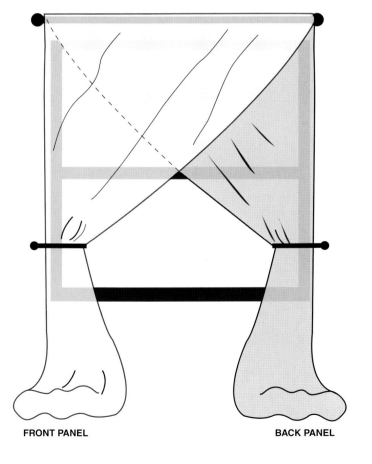

FRONT PANEL   BACK PANEL

Project notes

If the window is wide enough to require a center support on the drapery rod, you will need to create two separate panels, which will require approximately double the amount of fabric. If you choose to use a printed fabric for this project, you will need to create two separate panels regardless of the width of your window.

Steps

1 Start by measuring the width of your window and determining the finished width of the drapery treatment. If the width of the window is over 48 inches, you will require a center rod support. Select the drapery rod and install it on the wall 4 inches above the window trim. Make sure to use self-anchoring molly bolts to hold the weight of the drapery rod in place.

If you are using a printed fabric and can iron, you might consider using an iron-on adhesive tape to keep the selvage edges of your fabric folded over. It's a much crisper look.

TIP

2 If the drapery rod is shorter than 48 inches, measure for one panel of fabric. Measure from the floor to the rod, double that measurement and add 48 inches for pooling the fabric on the floor. If the rod uses a center support, you will need to calculate yardage for two separate panels. Simply measure from the floor to the rod, double your measurement and add an additional 48 inches for pooling the fabric on the floor. Double this measurment to make two panels. **Note:** *For printed fabrics, cut the fabric to the specified panel lengths and iron the selvages to the back side of the fabric.*

3 If your window requires two panels of fabric, fold the fabric panels over the drapery rod, one on each side of the center support, and pull them down until the ends meet. At the rod, spread the fabric evenly from the ends to the center support. When this is done, pull the fabric panels back and determine the mounting location of the tieback hardware or the cup hooks. Mark their locations and install.

4 If your window requires only one panel, cut the fabric to

From Shari

Since most decorator fabrics measure about 54 inches wide, if you really want a full, rich look at the windows, I suggest you go with two full panels, regardless of how wide your window is. If the window is more than 72 inches wide, you may want to consider using two panels per side to give the draperies the right amount of fullness.

the specified panel length. Fold the fabric over the rod and pull it down until the ends meet. Spread the fabric evenly on the rod from one end to the other. Pull the front portion of the panel to the left, and the back portion of the panel to the right and determine the location

of the tiebacks or cup hooks. Mark the placement and install.

5 Pool the excess fabric gently on the floor, folding all raw edges under so they are not visible. ∎

No-Sew Swag Window Topper

Now anyone and everyone can have beautiful swag treatments on their windows—all it takes is a little ironing, folding, stapling and hammering. Once your home is adorned with these elegant treatments, don't tell a soul that you never sewed a stitch!

Fabric

1x4 pine board cut to the width of the finished treatment

Two 3-inch L-brackets

¾-inch drywall screws

Iron-on adhesive tape for windows narrower than 44 inches

Staple gun and staples

Iron and ironing board

Rotary cutter or scissors

Cutting mat

Fabric measuring tape

Box nails

Cordless drill

Saw

Project note

Since the printed area of most decorator fabrics measures approximately 54–60 inches, this no-sew treatment can be used on windows measuring up to 46–52 inches. Eight inches of the fabric is used to wrap around the sides of the 1x4 board.

Steps

1 Measure and cut fabric to the length of the window plus 4 inches. For width, the fabric should be 8 inches wider than the width of the finished treatment.

2 Press out all of the wrinkles in the fabric, and press under ½ inch to the wrong side of fabric on both sides, including unprinted selvage edges.

3 With the pine board lying flat, line up the top edge of the fabric with the back edge of the pine board. The fabric should be covering the surface of the board. Center the fabric on the board so 3½ inches of fabric extends off both edges of the board. Use the staple gun to attach the fabric. Space staples every few inches, and add enough staples for the fabric to be secure.

4 Lift the board in the flat position. Wrap the 3½ inches of fabric around the end of the board, creating a fabric triangle (photo A). Fold triangle on top of board and staple in place (photo B). Repeat for other end.

Photo A

Photo B

From Shari

This is a fabulous look for non-sewers. If your window is larger, create two or three of these and butt them together as you attach them with L-brackets.

Another note: Striped patterns turn out wonderful with this treatment because the stripes curve softly with the swag and create a designer appearance!

5 With the fabric lying out flat, start with your hands at the bottom of the fabric, and begin fan-folding the fabric. The first fold has wrong sides of fabric folded together. The width of the folds should equal the width of the board, 3½ inches. Continue fan-folding until you get to the board.

6 With the board lying flat on the stapled side, adjust the folds to make it appear that all the folds are equal. Then use a couple of nails to tack the fabric to the board along the centerline of both the board and the fabric.

7 Flip the board over and watch the fabric hang down from the sides, meeting in the center to create a lovely swag design. You may have to again dress the folds.

8 Mount the L-brackets evenly spaced across the top of the window, with the bottom edge touching the top of the window frame. Center the new window treatment on top of the L-brackets and attach it using screws from the underside of the brackets into the 1x4. ∎

The length of this treatment is somewhat arbitrary. You want it to be long enough to be full and have plenty of pleats, but you will never lower it to cover the window, so it could be made shorter. Using 3½ inches as the width of a pleat, you could just cut the fabric at 59½ inches to make 8 pleats. This includes the one fold at the top which covers the top of the 1x4.

TIP

No-Sew Pleated Window Topper

Our first no-sew topper was so well received we had to come up with another one that's even better! This topper imitates a pleated valance with contrasting insets.

SHOPPING LIST

Main fabric for topper

Coordinating fabric for inside of pleats

Lining fabric to cover the pine board

1x4 pine board cut to the width of the finished treatment

2–3-inch L-brackets

¾-inch drywall screws

MATERIALS ON HAND

Staple gun and staples

Iron and ironing board

Fabric measuring tape

Calculator

Rotary cutter or scissors

Cutting mat

Cordless drill

Saw

Project notes

This particular project requires a bit of math, so you might want to grab a calculator for some quick figuring! These instructions list figures and measurements for a topper that is 48 inches wide and 14 inches long. It is made up of 9 flaps of the main fabric, 7 across the front at 6 inches wide and 2 on the sides at 3½ inches wide. There are also 8 flaps made out of the coordinating fabric that fall between the others. We chose to separate our main flaps by 1 inch to allow the coordinating fabric to be seen at all times.

Steps

1 Start by determining the width and height of your no-sew window topper. Keep in mind that most treatments are mounted 4 inches above the frame of the window, and extend a couple of inches past the framing on the sides.

2 Once you determine the width of your treatment, divide it into a number of even sections. These sections should range from about 4–12 inches wide. Ours were 6 inches wide and we needed 7 to cover the 48 inches of the topper, (figuring 1 inch between flaps). The topper will also require 2 additional flaps of the main fabric at 3½ inches wide to cover the ends of the 1x4.

3 For length, consider that a topper should measure about one fifth of the height of the window. Ours was 14 inches long.

4 To figure the cut size for the main fabric flaps, the length is the height determined in step 3 times 2 plus 7 inches. The width is the figure determined in step 2 plus 3 inches Cut as many of these out as needed to cover the front of the window. Cut two additional flaps out of the main fabric that measure the determined length and 6½ inches wide.

5 You will need to cut one less coordinating fabric flap than you did for the main fabric. These flaps are cut 2 inches shorter than the measurement figured in step 4 and are 6½ inches wide.

6 Once all the flaps are cut out, head over to the ironing board. First fold the long edges over 1½ inches and iron flat. Then, fold the entire flap in half with wrong sides facing and press the fold. Repeat this step for all the flaps. Two of the lining flaps then need to be folded in half lengthwise and ironed flat. They will be the corner flaps.

7 Cover the 1x4 board in lining fabric attached with staples.

8 Begin by attaching the coordinating fabric flaps. Start with the two on the corners. Line the flap up to just less than the length of the finished topper so they appear to recede. Fold the fabric over neatly and staple in place. Continue with the coordinating flaps, spacing them to fit nicely between the main fabric flap locations.

9 Staple the main fabric flaps over the others, allowing them to extend about ⅛ inch past them.

10 When all flaps are stapled in place, mount the board above the window using L-brackets. ∎

> **Lightweight cotton fabrics** work very nicely for this project because they iron up so crisp, making the flaps even more realistic as pleats.
>
> **TIP**

From Shari

The first time I tried this idea, I didn't separate the main fabric flaps, I butted them together. Unfortunately, the lovely coordinating fabric below was seen only when the window was open and a breeze was blowing in. So, I recommend leaving some of the coordinating fabric showing, since you've gone through all the work!

Tie-Up Valance

My initial plan with this simple valance was to get Matt involved, and while he sewed, I would relax! Well, after much deliberation with the sewing machine, Matt got an idea of his own … iron-on adhesive tape! He was right; this is just one of many window topper treatments you can create without the use of a sewing machine!

Fabric

**Sewing thread to match
  fabric, or iron-on
  adhesive tape**

**Coordinating grosgrain
  ribbon**

**Continental-style
  curtain rod**

MATERIALS ON HAND

**Tools for installing
  curtain rod**

Iron and ironing board

Sewing machine

Fabric measuring tape

Rotary cutter or scissors

Steps

1 Install drapery rod in desired position. Usually the top of the rod is 4 inches above the window trim.

2 Measure the width of the rod (plus the returns on both sides if needed). For a lightly gathered topper without any center seams, you may be able to use one width of decorator fabric (which can range from 54–60 inches wide). If additional fullness is desired, double the measurement of the rod which will require more than one width of fabric. (See below for optional piecing instructions).

Optional for wide windows: Cut two fabric panels to the necessary length. Cut one panel in half along the length of the fabric. Sew or use iron-on adhesive to attach a half-width panel to each side of the full-width panel. Keep in mind the width of the seams and side hems as you figure the width of cut panels (see Fig. 1).

3 To determine the length of the topper, decide whether or not you will lower the valance and how much of the window you wish to cover. If you would like a stationary valance, you may only need to add an additional 12 inches to create the lower edge detail. When figuring the fabric dimensions, do not forget to add extra for the hem and the rod pocket.

4 Sew or use iron-on adhesive to finish the outside edges of the fabric panel.

5 Fashion a rod pocket by sewing or with iron-on adhesive tape. Measure the thickness of the rod and add an additional ⅜ inches for the depth of the pocket. For instance, the pocket depth to best fit a 2½-inch rod is 2⅞ inches. This allows the pocket to fit neatly over the rod without being too tight or too loose.

6 Hem the bottom of the valance then slide it onto the rod.

7 The valance shown is tied up with two pieces of grosgrain ribbon, which makes a great country-style valance. For a different look, try using rope trim, coordinating fabric strips or embroidered ribbons. Use two ribbons as shown, or use one ribbon right in the center of the window for a simple-to-do swag. ∎

From Shari

All kidding aside, iron-on adhesive is a marvelous way to create seams and hems, and it allows people without sewing knowledge to create wonderful decorative projects for their homes. I keep a supply of it on hand at all times!

Half width of fabric	Full width of fabric	Half width of fabric

Fig. 1

It's best for this valance design to NOT sew a ruffle at the top of the pocket, which is often done. In this design, the ribbons will not lay neatly over a ruffle.

TIP

Reversible Valance

This reversible valance is a simple way to dress up plain, purchased sheers or draperies. In fact, this valance is simple enough to whip up quickly for the holidays, or for something as unique as a special treatment to display on a birthday or anniversary.

Project note

If your window is wide enough that the drapery rod requires a center support, consider a heavy-duty rod to eliminate the need for one. If you decide to stick with a center rod support, you will need to make two toppers separated in the center by the width of the center support. These instructions are for windows less than 54 inches wide.

Steps

1 Begin by installing the drapery rod over the existing draperies or blinds. At a minimum, the rod should be mounted to the wall 4 inches above the top of the draperies; however, at the sides it should protrude only about an inch or so from the current treatment so as not to look too wide.

2 When the rod is hung, determine the length of the reversible valance. Generally, the center is longer than the sides. We chose a simple V-shape for ours, but you can consider a soft curve or create your own shape using tissue paper to transfer the design to the fabric. Valances should be about one fifth of the length of the full drapery. The draperies shown in the photo measure 84 inches, and our drapery rod was positioned 4 inches above that, making the total length 88 inches, divided by 5, or 17.6 inches long. Of course we rounded to 18 inches for the back panel, and 15 inches for the front, which allows 3 inches of the reversible fabric to show from the front.

3 Add the two panel-length measurements together and add an additional ½ inch to 1½ inches, depending on the thickness of your drapery rod, to determine cutting length. Don't forget to add 1¼ inches for seam allowances. To determine the cut width of the valance, measure the length of the rod to be covered, making sure the entire drapery or blind will be covered, and add 1¼ inches for seam allowances. Cut two panels to these measurements, one from the front fabric and one from the coordinating fabric.

From Shari

If you don't want to add trims or tassels directly to the valance, you can always attach the tassels to a length of rope trim and drape the trim from one finial to the other, or just hang tassels at the ends of the rod for a dressy effect.

4 Place the two fabrics together, wrong sides facing, to create and cut out the decorative end designs. Again, we used a simple V-shape with a 3-inch variance from the center to the edges. This was easy to draw with a straightedge and cut out.

5 Pin the two panels together with right sides facing and sew around the outside edges, leaving a 6-inch opening along the middle of one of the sides for turning. Clip the corners of the selvages, trim the seams and turn the valance right side out.

6 Press the valance; pin and hand-stitch the opening closed. Add any desired trims or tassels at this time.

7 Fold the valance over the installed rod and adjust until you have just the right amount of

the coordinating fabric showing. Now try reversing the fabric—it looks great either way! ■

Café Awning

Wouldn't it be great to travel to a quaint little bistro somewhere in the Mediterranean for a romantic lunch? Well, Matt keeps insisting that you can get the same feeling right in your home by creating a bistro-style awning for the window in your dining room or breakfast nook. I think he's right!

SHOPPING LIST

Fabric

Sewing thread to match fabric

1 café curtain rod

1 café curtain rod with extra-long returns

Iron-on shade interfacing

Coordinating decorative trim (optional)

MATERIALS ON HAND

Tools for installing curtain rods

Measuring tape

Iron and ironing board

Pencil

Cardboard for scallop and side-angle templates

Fabric measuring tape

Sewing machine

Hot glue gun and glue sticks

Project note

It's easier to install the café rods in their positions and then measure for the amount of fabric needed to purchase than trying to figure it all out beforehand. Also, this awning is made running the fabric the length of the café rod to eliminate having to piece the flat area of the awning together, so choose your fabric accordingly.

Steps

1 As with any window treatment, decide how the awning will be positioned. Usually, a treatment like this looks best if installed an inch or so beyond the wood frame on each side and 2–4 inches above the top of the window frame. Install the upper curtain rod in this position. **Note:** *Try to find a rod that will keep the top of the awning as close to the wall as possible. If you want the awning to actually touch the wall, you could use a flat café rod like the ones used on doors.*

2 Next, install the lower curtain rod with the extended returns at a level where you'd like the awning to break before the scallops begin. The distance between the two rods and the length of the side returns on the bottom rod is what creates the angle of the awning. The further down you install the bottom rod, the steeper the angle will be.

3 Measure to get a general feel for the size of the awning so that you know how much fabric

and interfacing to purchase. Measure the approximate width of the awning, and add a few inches, (this is the approximate length of fabric required). Then measure the height and add a few inches to be sure your fabric is wide enough. Be sure you purchase enough fabric and iron-on shade interfacing to cut out a long awning piece with scallops and two side panels.

4 Begin the awning by ironing the shade interfacing to the back of the fabric panel according to the manufacturer's instructions.

5 To get the final cutting measurements, start at the top edge of the top rod and measure down and over the bottom rod to the place you'd like the scallops to end. To this measurement, add enough to form the rod pocket for the top rod. (For a 1-inch café rod, this would be an additional 3½ inches for the pocket and the seam allowance to provide enough ease for the curtain to fit over the rod. You will not need to add anything additional for a hem since the bottom will be cut off and finished in scallops. For the

From Shari
So what do you think? It may not be quite the same as visiting the Mediterranean, but I can guarantee, it's less expensive!

width, measure the exact length of the rod and add 1¼ inches for seam allowances. Cut out a piece of fabric to this measurement. Trim a ⅝-inch notch in each upper corner of the fabric the length of the measurement of the rod pocket (see Fig. 1).

6 Fold over the rod pocket so the stitch lines match and sew it in place. Then temporarily hang the awning to create a template for the side pieces.

7 To draw a template for the angled side pieces, hold a piece of cardboard flush against the wall and the open side of the awning. Draw the angle and length of the side piece to fit. Add a ⅝-inch seam allowance to the angled edge of the template and cut out (see Fig. 2.) Trace around the outside edge of the template on the interfaced side of a piece of fabric. Flip the template and trace another triangle on the interface side of the fabric. Cut out both triangles. Remove the awning from the rod and sew the angled sides to the straight sides of the awning front. Trim the seam allowances and press.

8 Determine the size of the scallops keeping in mind the full length of the awning, including the side pieces, and cut a template of about 3 to 4 scallops. Usually 4–6 inches wide is a nice dimension for scallops. Mark the center of the template. Place the center of the template at the bottom center back of the awning and draw around the curved edge of the template onto the interfacing. Draw scallops evenly across the bottom edge of the awning. Cut out the scalloped edge.

9 If using trim, hot glue trim over the raw edges of the scallop on the front face of the awning.

10 Hang the awning, pulling it down gently over the bottom rod to shape. ■

Many awnings are done in vertical stripes, and that would be difficult to do the way these instructions are written. Just keep in mind that you can piece the front panel with widths of fabric, or if you're lucky, the window won't require additional widths at all!

TIP

⅝"

½"   3½"

stitch line

stitch line

FABRIC

Fig. 1
Notches for Rod Pocket

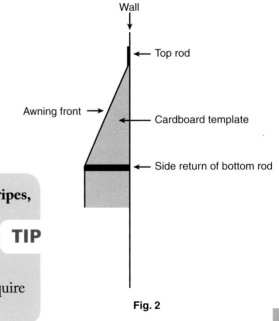

Wall

Top rod

Awning front →   Cardboard template

Side return of bottom rod

Fig. 2

Mock Swag & Jabot Topper

It's hard to believe that a simple flat curtain panel can create the feel of a swag and jabot. If you're looking for an unstructured, yet dressy look for your windows, this topper just may be the answer.

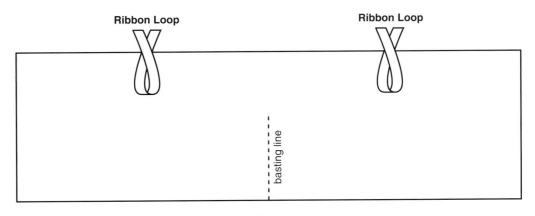

Fig. 1
Loop Placement

Project note

These instructions are written for windows up to 36 inches wide. Larger windows will require a center drawer pull and loop for extra support as well as more than one cut of fabric for width.

Steps

1 Begin by installing the drawer pulls on the wall or on the window trim in the desired location. If they are mounted on the wall, spacers the depth of the window trim and painted to match the walls are recommended. If they are mounted on the trim, place the pulls on the top left and top right corners.

2 Windows measuring 36 inches or less will require one full width of fabric 54 inches wide or wider to cover the width of this treatment. Cut both fabrics to the same width, removing the selvage edges and only enough of the printed area of the wider fabric to make the two pieces identical. For cut length, measure from the bottom of the drawer pull to the point you'd like the center of the topper to end. Add 1¼ inches to this measurement for seams.

3 Measure the distance between the drawer pulls, and center this measurement along the top edge of one of the panels, marking where the fabric will meet the pulls. At the markings, pin on loops made of ribbon, cord or coordinating fabric to loop over the drawer pulls. Make sure that the loop is facing down onto the fabric and the cut ends are up in the seam allowance.

4 With right sides facing, pin the coordinating fabric to the first fabric and stitch around the outside edges, leaving a 6-inch area unstitched to turn the topper right side out.

5 Remove the pins, clip the corners and trim the seam allowances. Turn the topper right side out and iron flat.

6 Hand-stitch the opening closed.

7 To create the swag, measure the width and mark the center point along the bottom edge. With a needle and doubled thread, and using large basting stitches, baste from the bottom edge, up towards the top edge about 6 to 8 inches. Pull on the thread to pull the fabric up and create a mock swag. When you have the fabric pulled up enough to satisfy, use the remaining doubled thread to sew on a button in this location to hold the swag in place. Hang your new mock swag and jabot. ■

From Shari

For a fun detail, sew coordinating cord along the bottom of the topper, and then use matching drapery pull backs, tied in a loop, knotted and hand-stitched to the front side of the topper as the loops for hanging over the drawer pulls. Another option is to hang tassels on both sides of the pulls for a pretty detail.

Embellished Flat Panels

When it comes to window treatments, the sky is the limit. However, sometimes our time is limited. Embellishing store-bought flat curtain panels is a great way to add a personal touch to your window treatments without starting from scratch. Read along … this is one window treatment you'll definitely want to try.

SHOPPING LIST

Purchased flat curtain panels (if needed)

Main fabric for embellishment

Contrasting fabric

Purchased piping

Sewing thread to match fabrics

MATERIALS ON HAND

Measuring tape

Sewing machine

Fabric measuring tape

Cutting mat

Straightedge

Rotary cutter or scissors

Pins

Steps

1 Hang store-bought flat curtain panels at desired height. Consider where you would like to place an embellishment, and what size you would like. A contrasting strip could have just as easily been added to the top of the curtain as to the bottom.

2 Our bottom addition measured 21 inches high, approximately one fifth of the total height of the curtain, and it was the same width as the panel.

3 Start by cutting the main embellishment fabric to the width of the curtain panel plus the same amount of side seams as is on the curtain. Ours was 40 inches wide plus 1½ inches side seams for a total of 6 additional inches, or 46 inches wide. For the length of the embellishment, 3 inches of the 21 inches was a contrasting fabric and piping, so 18 inches plus a ⅝-inch seam allowance and a 4-inch hem folded twice is 26⅝ inches in length.

4 Cut the contrasting fabric for the embellishment at the same width as in step 3 (46 inches) and 4¼ inches in length, which includes the ⅝-inch seam allowances.

5 Cut length of piping to same measurement as width in step 3 (46 inches).

6 Pin piping on right side of main fabric along the top edge. Place contrasting fabric, right side down onto piping and pin. Stitch all three layers of fabric together using a zipper foot on your machine.

7 Fold over side hems 1½ inches twice, and use same stitch as side seams on flat curtain panels. Make sure when this is done that the new embellishment is the same width as the flat curtain panel.

8 Fold up 4-inch hem twice on embellishment and blind-stitch or straight-stitch in place.

9 Cut the curtain panel across the width at the location of the embellishment making sure to leave a ⅝-inch seam allowance. Pin the embellishment to the cut edge of the curtain panel with right sides facing and stitch together.

10 Make a flat-felled seam where the two panels join to neaten up the ends of the seams where the two fabrics meet.

11 Press curtains and re-hang. ∎

From Shari

If you don't want to cut your original flat panel curtains, you can cheat the way I did. For the contrasting stripe on the embellishment, I folded the strip over in half and then added it to the main fabric and piping. This made it a bit sturdier. Then, I attached the embellished piece to the flat panel using straight pins. I just wove them in and out of the curtain and the contrasting stripe as if I was sewing with straight pins. I don't think you can tell, and it does preserve the original curtains in case I decide to add something different for the holidays or a special occasion!

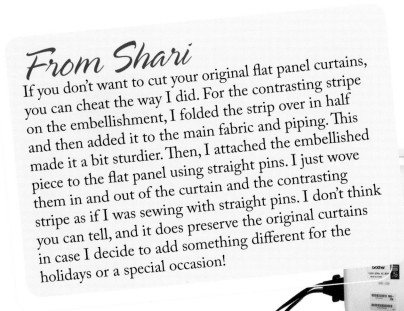

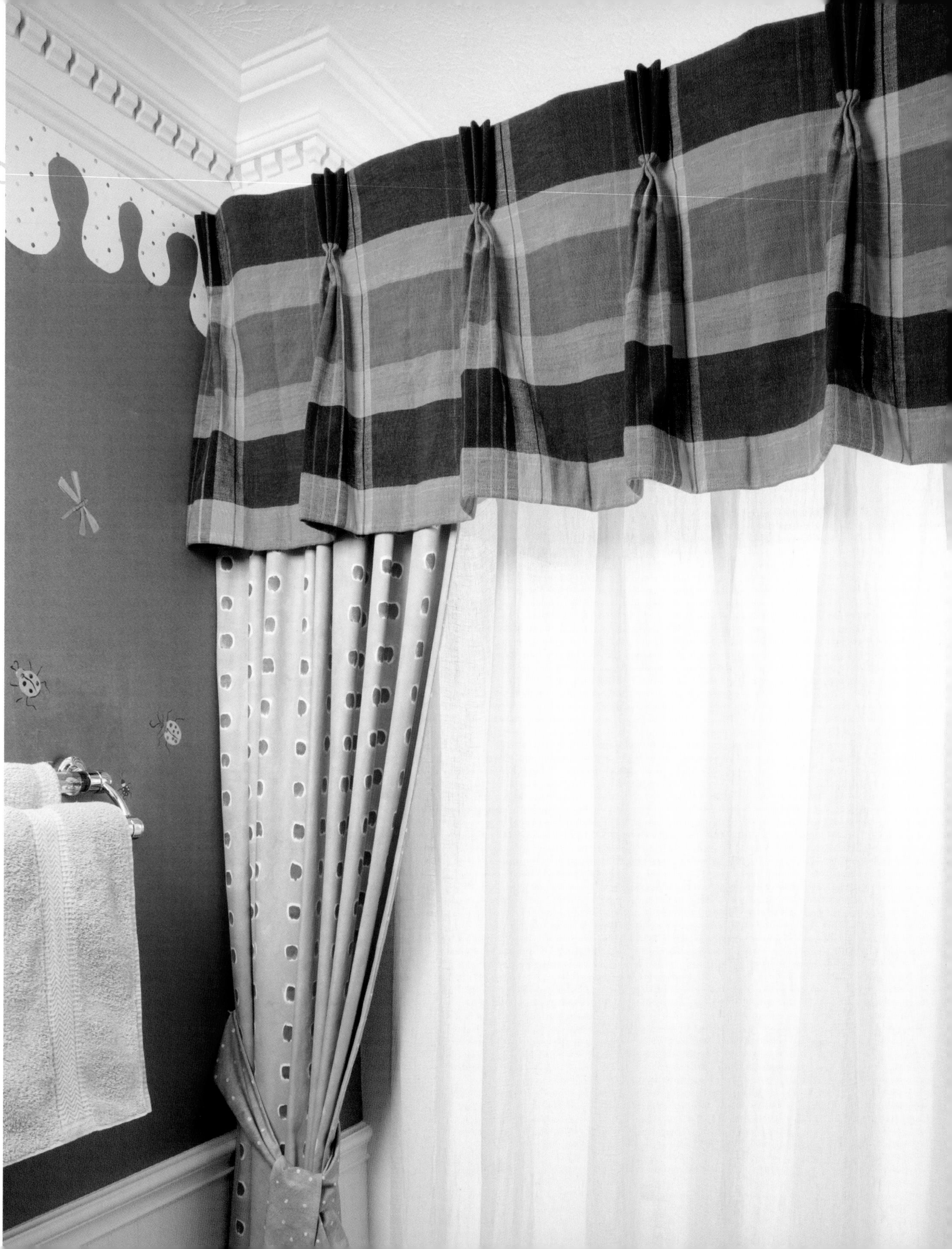

Layered Shower Curtain

Add a fresh new look to your bathroom with a colorful, layered treatment! The pinch-pleated valance is the most time-consuming part of this project, but once you get the hang of making the pleats, they're easy and fun, and add a tailored look to the valance. Now take a deep breath—this project takes some time, but the results will bring compliments for years to come!

Project notes

Our layered bathtub curtain treatment consists of four separate pieces: 1) the plastic liner that hangs inside the bathtub and protects the fabric layers from moisture, 2) the pleated fabric curtain that hangs outside the tub, 3) the side panel that is tied back, and 4) the pinch-pleated, lined valance. Shower-curtain measurements are standard, and specific cutting dimensions are given for this project, but feel free to adapt these instructions for curtains to fit the style of your bathroom.

Steps

1 Determine the height of the valance and side panel first, then install the café rods at the height of the drapery pins (approximately 1 inch lower than the top of the valance). Leave about 2 inches of space between the rods. The round tension rod for the plastic liner can be put up at any time since it simply tightens into place.

Pleated fabric curtain

1 Cut and piece the fabric until you have a piece that is 124 inches wide by 82 inches high.

To keep seams from detracting from the look of the curtain, use a full width of fabric for the center panel and cut panels to fit on both sides of the center, bringing the pieced fabric to the proper width. Fold the top edge over 2 inches twice for the top hem; iron and pin in place. Fold the bottom edge up 3 inches twice for the bottom hem; sew in place. Fold each side edge over 1 inch twice and sew in place.

2 Fold and pin soft pleats in the top of the fabric curtain every 6 inches as shown in Fig. 1 starting 3 inches in from the edge. When pleats are pinned, hold the top of fabric curtain against the plastic liner to be sure pleats fall in line with the hook holes in the plastic liner. Readjust pleat positions if necessary and re-pin. Sew pleats in place along top hemline and ¼ inch in from top edge. Mark positions of holes on fabric curtain so plastic liner is lower at the top and can't be seen. (Grommets on fabric curtain will be placed lower to accommodate this.) Install a grommet in each marked position.

3 Install shower curtain rings through fabric curtain and plastic liner, and hang curtain with plastic liner placed inside tub. Reposition rod if necessary so that fabric curtain ends about 2 inches up from the floor outside the tub.

Side panel & tieback

1 Cut one side panel, 40 inches wide by 92 inches long. Fold over each side edge 1 inch twice and sew in place. Fold over top edge ½ inch and then 1½ inches for top rod pocket; sew in place. Fold up bottom edge 3 inches twice for bottom hem; sew in place. Place panel on middle café rod and

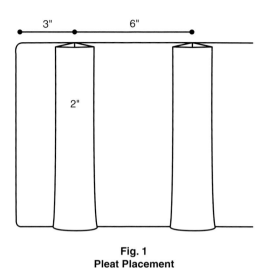

Fig. 1
Pleat Placement

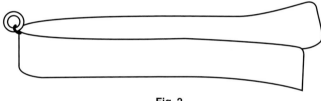

Fig. 2
Ring Placement

gather to take up approximately 18 inches of the rod.

2 Measure approximately 45 inches up from floor and place a mark on the wall at this height in the location where the panel touches the wall. Install cup hook in this position.

3 For tieback, cut one piece of fabric, 49 inches by 7 inches. Fold piece in half lengthwise and sew ½-inch seams across the bottom short edge and up long side to form a tube; trim. Turn the tube right side out. Fold ½ of raw

edge of tube to inside and sew opening closed. Press the tube flat, fold in half and sew a ring to this position as shown in Fig. 2.

4 Hang ring of tieback on cup hook and softly tie ends of tieback around side panel. Dress folds neatly.

Pinch-pleat valance
Note: *Our valance had to cover a span of 68 inches so determining the position of the pleats may be different on your valance. Basically, divide the distance to be covered by the amount of*

space you want between pleats, we used 8 inches. So, 68 inches divided by 8 equals 8½, so there will be 8 spaces of 8 inches (meaning 9 pleats) and the leftover 4 inches is divided between the two ends. The instructions below use measurements and figures to create a valance that is 68 inches wide and 20 inches high.

1 Cut and piece fabric to measure 112½ inches wide by 34 inches high. Cut and piece lining fabric to measure 112½ inches wide by 20 inches high. With wrong sides together and

> **You may want to use pleater tape** to create the three-prong pleats. It's a fast and easy way if you are a beginner. Just ask your local drapery professional to show you how to use it.
>
> **TIP**

lining placed 8 inches down from the upper edge of the valance, lay 4 inches buckram just above top edge of lining. Fold 4 inches of the valance fabric over the buckram and then fold it another 4 inches to cover the top of the lining fabric. Pin in place.

2 Fold each end of both the valance lining and fabric over 1 inch twice and sew in place.

3 On the right side of the valance, mark the positions of the pleats. For ours we started at one end and marked off 2 inches, then 4½ inches for a pleat, then 8 inches for a space and so on.

4 Fold each pleat by bringing the pleat lines together with the pleat to the front of the valance. Pin in place and crease buckram on the center fold. Stitch along pleat line from the top of the heading to the lower edge of the buckram. Secure by backstitching.

5 Divide each pleat into three even pleats by opening the pleat at the top of the heading and pinching the center pleat in your fingers. Press the center pleat straight down to meet the pleat stitching line and new pleats will be created at the sides. Crease the buckram at these new pleats.

6 Pull outer folds up to meet the center fold and finger-press the pleats together making sure they are all even. Bar-tack the pleats just above the edge of the buckram to hold them in place.

7 After the pleats are in position, fold the bottom of the valance up 3 inches twice to form the hem; sew in place.

8 Insert a drapery pin in each pleat and hang the valance on the outside rod. ∎

From Shari

This shower curtain design can be easily adapted for any style of decorating. For a warm country look, use two coordinating fabric prints and sew a scallop in the bottom of the panel. For a traditional room, try combining a subtle stripe with a matching floral print. No matter what style you choose, a layered shower curtain makes any bathroom look like a million bucks!

ACCESSORY PROJECTS

There are two ways to look at accessories: They can either be the final touch that brings a room to life, or they can be the springboard for an entire room redecoration. Either way, a home isn't complete without them!

Decorating a Mantel

In earlier times, the fireplace was the center of family life. That isn't surprising, since the fireplace was the source of food, light and warmth. Times have changed, but a fireplace is still an important decorating element in many homes.

In fact, a fireplace is the focal point of a room, and it deserves special attention. Collect an interesting assortment of artwork to decorate the wall above the fireplace, and then add other coordinating items to the mantel to complete the look!

When you decorate a fireplace, you are really decorating two distinct areas—the wall above the fireplace and the mantel. Before you begin, study the decor in the rest of the room. The theme of the room should help you determine the types of accessories to use. These items should reflect the style and color palette of the room and coordinate with the dominant theme.

Traditionally, the wall area above the mantel is used to display a large piece of artwork. When choosing artwork for this space, scale is very important. If you are living in a home where the space above the mantel is four feet or less, a large painting or mirror is a good choice. For a different look, place the artwork on the mantel and lean it against the wall instead of hanging it.

In newer homes, choosing artwork for the area above a mantel can be a challenge. Great rooms with soaring two-story ceilings are often the norm in new construction, which means this wall space above a fireplace can be about 15 feet tall!

A single piece of art can work in this instance, if the piece is very large—huge, in fact. Since art of this size can be pricey, you may wish to consider the alternative of creating a grouping of smaller items.

Obviously it is possible to create a large group of small paintings. To unify the look, they should share the same theme or perhaps be matted and framed in a similar manner. But who said the only thing you can hang on a wall is a picture? Almost anything can be used to create a grouping. Interesting textiles, including tapestries or quilts, can make an eye-catching statement above a fireplace.

Many people hang a large mirror above the mantel, but what about hanging a collection of different sizes of mirrors instead?

Architectural pieces, including antique windows, shutters or gingerbread trim can be combined for a unique grouping. Groupings of pretty plates and platters are another option. Whether old or new, they provide color and depth to a plain wall.

Creating a grouping can be quite time-consuming, so it is important to have a plan. Unless you love filling in holes, the place to plan

the grouping is on the floor, not the wall. Mark off an area of the floor that is the same size as the area above the fireplace. Experiment with the placement of the items in the group, balancing larger items with several smaller ones.

When you are satisfied with the arrangement, make a sketch of the items, noting sizes of the items, spaces between them and location of hangers. Using these measurements, mark the placement of the items on the wall. Or, another easy method is to cut the shapes and sizes of the items you plan on hanging out of newspaper or brown paper bags. Then you can move them around the wall space, taping them in place to stand back and get a better feel for your arrangement. Then just measure off of the templates to place the nails and hooks!

Make sure to check the weight of each item to determine the proper hanging method. Apply the hangers to the wall and place the items on the hangers. Hopefully your plans were accurate and the grouping looks just like you envisioned. But wait—you still aren't finished. You still need to decorate the mantel!

Once again, the mantel arrangement should support the style of the room. In a traditional room, it is common to use a

symmetrical arrangement, while in a more casual or modern setting, an asymmetrical design may be preferred.

Since mantel accessories should complement the wall grouping and not compete with it, you'll be happy to know mantel decor can be kept to a minimum. Candles, candlesticks, vases and greenery are all good choices for a mantel.

To create visual interest, vary the size and elevation of the objects you choose.

While today's fireplaces are no longer used as the primary source of food, heat and light, they still can be the family gathering place in your home. With a beautiful wall grouping and mantel display, the fireplace will become an area that naturally attracts attention! ■

Table Scapes & Vignettes

Creating vignettes for tabletops, shelves and other horizontal surfaces
doesn't have to be a daunting task. Keep the style of the room in
mind while planning placement of accessories and before you know
it you'll have a decorated surface that complements your decor.

There are really no hard and fast rules for creating a grouping of accessories on a dresser top, counter, shelf or window ledge. The first step is to address functional issues of both the flat surface and the main vignette piece. For example, is there a need for a light source on top of a dresser? If so, build the vignette around a lamp.

When functional needs are decided upon, look at the overall design of the room. For effective table-scaping, the accessories must support the style and theme of the room. If the room is formal, symmetrical groupings work best. For informal rooms, asymmetrical arrangements are ideal.

The vignettes should help coordinate the room in which they are placed. One way to do this is through color. Choose items that complement the dominant room color. Same-color accessories in different shades of that color can also be used to create an attractive grouping. Silk flowers or artificial fruit are a great way to introduce color into a grouping.

For visual interest, display an odd number of items. Groups of items have more visual impact than a single object. Combinations of

three to five work particularly well. Be careful, though, not to display too many items. Three or five accessories are interesting to look at, while too many items may appear cluttered.

When creating a grouping, place similar objects together—grouped according to size, shape or color. To add visual interest, vary the height of the objects. If necessary, place some items on small pedestals or stands to elevate

them. A stack of books makes a great stand for smaller objects.

When choosing items for a grouping, it sometimes helps to stick to one theme. For instance, create a grouping of candles of varying heights, or display framed photos of family vacations. If your favorite vacation spot happens to be the beach, add a seashell to support the theme.

Create depth in a grouping by alternating pieces from back to front instead of placing them in a straight line. Try placing three items in a triangular arrangement with the tallest pieces in back. Overlap the triangles if displaying more than three objects.

Mirrors make a great addition to a room, even if used on a flat surface such as a tabletop or the top of a dresser. Items placed on top of the mirror become more dimensional and interesting. For a touch of the unexpected, try leaning a smaller framed mirror against a larger mirror.

Ornamental shelving can be a challenge to decorate. Most units have five or six shelves—that's a lot of vignettes! Decorating

the shelves in a zigzag pattern can make the process less intimidating. On one shelf, place the tallest item on the far left; place the tallest item on the next shelf on the far right.

To make a display even more attractive, vary the textures of the items in the grouping. Architectural elements of wood or iron can add character to a shelf. Photos in a variety of frame styles can become a focal point.

Use greenery to add texture and softness to a vignette. Tuck some silk greenery into a corner of a shelf while trailing a second piece

over the edge of another shelf. Or fill a basket with silk greenery and make it a focal point by placing it in the center of a shelf.

Placing vignettes in the kitchen takes a bit more consideration than arranging a vignette on a dresser. The first step is to put away all of the accessories and small appliances that may currently reside on the counter. Decide what your kitchen is trying to tell you—are the colors rustic and calling for country or outdoorsy accessories? Would French-country roosters add a touch of whimsy? Would contemporary, colored-glass vases or bottles look best?

Once you have an idea of what your kitchen is trying to say, select a theme name—the more descriptive, the better. The name you decide on will help determine the type of accessories to use. For instance, a "sophisticated fruit basket" theme rules out rustic baskets made from twigs, but allows a complex, woven basket that may include wrought iron or stamped metalwork. When the theme is set, it's time to get the functional items squared away before you begin shopping for accessories.

Return the small appliances to their previous places on the counters, along with functional items such as canister sets, knife blocks, paper-towel holders, etc. This is a good time to be brutal—decide what you really need on the counter for convenience. Place all remaining items in cabinets.

Carefully determine how you move through the kitchen. Place the remaining items on the counter in the best spot for that activity. Think this through—your kitchen should operate like a well-oiled

machine. Take note of the empty spaces and any wall outlets that could be hidden by sliding over an appliance or a well-placed accessory. Note, too, any bare wall spaces that could hold artwork. Measure the space, both linear and vertical, over the cabinets. With this information in hand, you're ready to choose accessories.

For above the cabinets, you have a few arrangement possibilities. Fill the entire area with a variety of heights and shapes of items, tied together by color or theme, or garlands of greenery and berries. If that seems too much for the space, create vignettes of accessories placed in strategic locations, with bare spots in between for added drama. Do not arrange items in a line across the tops of the cabinets—this lacks rhythm and interest.

For countertops, place a few theme-related accessories in out-of-the–way places. Use a small picture, plate or cookbook on a stand to hide unsightly outlets. Items that are functional as well as decorative are perfect for countertop decorating. Think pitchers, spice racks, bowls, canisters and salt-and-pepper shakers. Do allow some empty space on the countertops to

prevent a cluttered, crowded feeling.

Arranging a vignette in any room can take time—sometimes a great deal of time. The final result is more than worth the time and effort, because these are the personal touches that will make your home warm, unique and all about YOU! ∎

Hanging Artwork—Creating a Collage

Once you learn the basics of hanging artwork, you'll quickly advance to the "pro" level and will be able to create unique collage wall displays!

Hanging one piece of artwork is easy compared to putting together a collage of pieces and hanging them in just the right combination and location to make the collage work. Start with the basics to learn how to properly hang one piece of framed artwork.

Determine where the piece of framed art will hang. Eye level is a general rule. While you're holding the piece up to the wall, have someone else place a tiny pencil mark on the wall at the center of the top of the frame. Next, lean the picture against your legs and hook one finger of each hand around

the hanging wire, as if your fingers are the hanging hooks. Have your helper measure: 1) the distance between your fingers, and 2) how far down your fingers are from the top of the frame. Commit these measurements to memory (or jot them down on a scrap of paper). Now go back to the pencil mark

on the wall. Measure down from the mark the distance your fingers were from the top of the frame and mark this location on the wall. Now divide the measurement from finger to finger by 2. Note this location on a tape measure. For instance, if the distance from finger to finger is 10 inches, 10 divided by 2 equals 5, which is the center point between the two hooks. Place the tape measure in position with the 5-inch mark at the second pencil dot on the wall. Mark 0 inches and 10 inches on the wall. These marks denote the placement of the hanging hooks. To be completely precise, use a level with a ruled edge.

Now that you've mastered hanging individual pieces of artwork, you are ready to tackle a wall collage. A collage is a group of related items hung together on a wall to create a more dynamic statement than if each piece was hung alone. To get started, gather some items that have something in common with each other—all black and white photographs, or gold-framed artwork, for instance. Add a few coordinating dimensional items, such as a gold candle sconce, a gold-framed mirror, a hanging glass container

In the photo on the left, the staggered arrangement of four pictures gains extra interest and movement from the unusual layout alone. The wallpaper depicts a gardening theme, and the brown background of the pictures accents it nicely.

Right and below, easy-to-make fabric bows seem to accessorize the accessories! The blue bow brings out the blue of the sky in the Tom Caldwell print. A bow can even tie two or more framed pieces together, with a little style.

of potpourri or a coordinating clock. Don't overdo the variety so much that the common theme of the grouping is lost.

Make a conscious effort to bring together subjects that tell a story. For instance, floral prints combined with dragonfly and ladybug artwork make sense because of the subject matter. The frames can be different, yet they'll all still get along together on the wall. Another great collage unifier is color. If all the prints in a collage grouping are watercolors, or pen and ink, they will make a cohesive display when hung as a group.

Framed photographs make a great basis for interesting wall collages. When creating a grouping with photos, it is important that each piece be a part of the whole. There are several ways to achieve a unified look. One way to maintain collage consistency with photographs is to group the photos by color. Black and white photos can create a modern-gallery look. Sepia tones work well with traditional and country decor. Full-color photos are best displayed in a casual setting. Photos can also be grouped by theme—vacations, family members or special occasions, for example.

When the collage items have been collected, start arranging them on the floor using a space the same size as the available wall space. Using the floor makes it much easier to move things around and get a feel for the overall effect. Don't forget to include all the items you've collected. If something doesn't seem to fit in, save it to use on another wall in a different room. Keep in mind that collages do not need to be symmetrical. Often the items are arranged in an overall oval, rectangle or circular shape.

This rectangular arrangement makes no attempt to hide its theme: shells! The addition of three-dimensional shells on the shelf below really brings the artwork to life.

Black and white photography looks fabulous matted in white and framed in black. To bring even more attention to the pieces, we added a trim molding to the wall and painted the inset to contrast with the blue-gray walls of the room.

From Shari

All photographs will fade in time with exposure to light, heat and humidity. If you want to display vintage photographs, consider having photocopies made to frame instead of the original photo. The precious family heirlooms can then be stored in an archival box to prevent damage and aging. Ask the assistant at the copy store to photocopy a black and white photo on a color machine for the best-quality reproduction. It's a bit more expensive, but well worth it for the difference in the finished copy.

Moving the collage from the floor to the wall may seem overwhelming, but it's really very easy. Use a pencil to trace the outside edge of each item on brown grocery sacks or kraft paper, and then cut out each item. Transfer the paper item to the wall, using painter's blue tape to prevent damaging the wall surface. What's nice about this technique is that you can move things around easily without having to move the nails over a smidge to get the artwork in the right position.

When everything is taped to the wall and has been tweaked as necessary, locate the hanging apparatus on each piece of artwork and transfer the location to its paper twin. You can actually nail the hangers right through the paper because it will tear away fairly easily.

Don't let high ceilings or large blank walls intimidate you. Just use larger art pieces to create the collage, and let the accessories on higher furniture add extra interest to the grouping. ■

This collage is a collection of timepieces.
Collages are not always symmetrical especially
if the pieces collected are different sizes.

This arrangement of four pages from a Victorian paper-doll kit
is embellished with a simple stenciled bow on the wall. The
matting is fabric, to tie in with the theme of the artwork.

Here's oval again, with a lovely timepiece taking
center stage. The green in the plates picks up
similar colors throughout the room while displaying
part of this homeowner's plate collection.

French Message Board

Place a message board in a kitchen or office to help keep track of all the important things that need to be remembered. While cork bulletin boards or dry-erase boards are functional, this style of message board makes a real decorating statement!

Project note

Homasote works well for this project because it is rigid enough to hang without warping, but pliant enough to accept tacks or pins. Homasote is also easily cut to a custom size or shape.

Steps

1 Cut the Homasote board to the desired size using a sharp utility knife and a straightedge. Cut a piece of quilt batting the same size as the board. Cut a piece of fabric 3 inches larger all the way around than the size of the board. A 24-inch-square memo board requires a 30-inch-square piece of fabric.

2 Spray the front of the board with a coat of adhesive. The surface of the board is very porous, so this first coat will help seal the board. When the adhesive is dry to the touch, spray a second coat. Carefully place the piece of quilt batting on the adhesive, making sure the batting is flat.

3 Lay the fabric right side down on a table, and place the batting side of the homosote board in the center of the fabric. Wrap the fabric around to the back of the board at the top and staple it in place. Next wrap the bottom and staple. Then move on to the sides. Pull the fabric taut, but not so much that the weave of the fabric is distorted.

4 Cut away the excess fabric at the corners of the board and fold it neatly, stapling the fabric to the back of the board.

5 Place satin ribbons on the face of the board in a diagonal pattern. We made sure that ribbons touched all four corners of the board and then arranged the rest of the ribbons accordingly. Wrap the ends to the back of the board and staple in place. Where the ribbons intersect on the front of the board, create a staple "x" to hold the ribbons tight.

6 Using coordinating thread, wrap the thread in the buttonholes of the buttons as if

From Shari

I'm using this very message board in my office right now, and my only regret is that I didn't make it bigger!

you have sewn them to a piece of fabric. Then hot-glue the buttons at the intersections of the ribbons.

7 Spray the back of the board with adhesive and cover with gift wrap or plain brown paper.

8 Attach a sawtooth hanger to the center top of the back of the board. ∎

Chalkboard

Create a chalkboard to match your decor by adding a thin plywood panel to the back of a purchased picture frame. Chalkboard paint finishes this project nicely, making it a perfect message center for an office or family room.

Project note

Luaun plywood is thin and can be cut with a utility knife. Hold a straightedge on the cutting line and score the wood until you have completely cut through. Do not try to break the plywood after only a few cuts—it will splinter and the surface will not be smooth.

Steps

1 Use the pliers to bend the metal tabs on the back of the frame out of the way. Remove the glass and backing from the frame.

2 Cut a 16x20-inch piece of luaun plywood. Sand edges until smooth.

3 Apply chalkboard paint to plywood in the direction of the grain. Let dry for four hours and apply a second coat.

4 Install chalkboard in frame, securing it by bending metal tabs back in position. ∎

TIPS

Save the glass from the picture frame to use in other projects. Wrap the edges with cardboard taped in place to prevent damage to the glass (and your fingers) while in storage.

This chalkboard can be made in other sizes. Purchase a premade frame in the desired size, and cut the plywood to the same measurement as the glass or backing.

Hang it in a spot everyone will see. The first note should read, "I made the board; someone else needs to make dinner!"

From Matt

Luaun plywood has a grainy texture. If you prefer a smoother texture, try using birch plywood or masonite, using a sharp utility knife or a table saw to cut the wood to size.

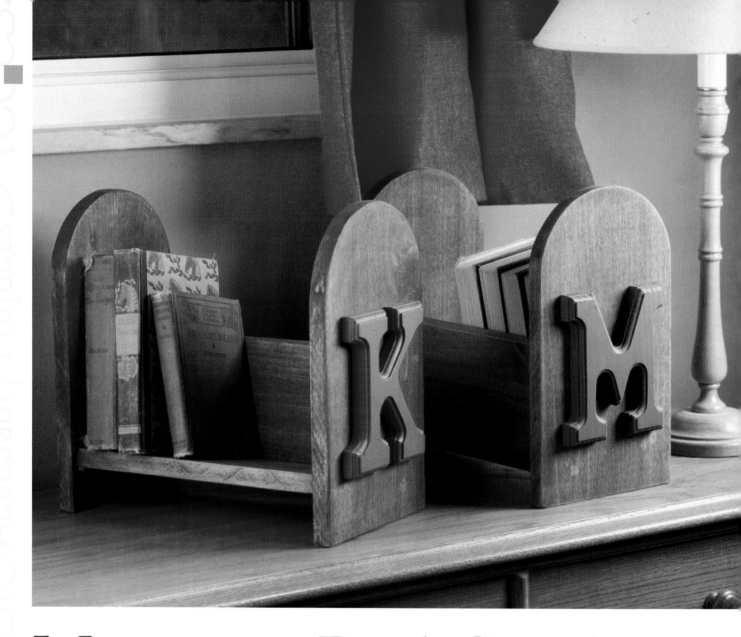

Monogram Book Stand

Monograms and initials are stylish decorating items. This free-standing book stand is a great way to display treasured volumes and a trendy initial. As a bonus, it can be finished for a den or office as well as for a child's room, simply by changing the finishing technique.

Project note

A jigsaw with a scroll blade makes a fine, clean cut that works best for cutting curves.

Steps

1 Use the circular saw and cutting guide to rip and cut two pieces of poplar, each 10x14 inches.

2 For the two ends, measure and mark the center top of each board. **Note:** *The center point should be 5 inches, but measure for accuracy and make a note of the measurement. Instructions will refer to 5 inches as the measurement, but use whatever measurement matches the center point of the lumber you are using.* From the top mark, measure down 5 inches and mark the board, making sure this mark is square with the top mark. Open the compass to 5 inches and set the point on the second mark. Draw a curve from one side of the board to the top center mark to the second side. Cut out the curve using the jigsaw with a scroll blade. Sand the top curves smooth first with 150-grit and then with 220-grit sandpaper.

3 For the shelf, use the circular saw and cutting guide to rip the remaining poplar to two 5½-inch widths (use a table saw if available) then cut each piece to 12 inches. Create an L-shape by butt-joining the two pieces together along the length using wood glue and finish nails. Let dry.

4 Place the L-shaped shelf between the end pieces at a slight angle to hold the books. Drill pilot holes into the shelf ends and attach with glue and finish nails. Let dry.

5 Fill all holes with wood putty. Allow to dry; sand flush. Stain or prime and paint the book stand in the color of your choice.

6 To personalize the book stand, paint or stain precut wooden letter as desired; let dry. Attach the letter to the side of the book stand with wood glue and finish nails; let dry.

7 Apply two coats of polyurethane to finished book stand. ■

> **Allow the last coat of polyurethane** to dry for at least 24 hours to prevent books from sticking to the stand.
>
> **TIP**

From Matt

Purchase wood filler that matches the stain and apply it after the stain has dried. The filler goes on flush, which eliminates the need for sanding. Most stain manufacturers will provide fillers that match their stain-product lines.

This is a great beginning wood project that you and your child will enjoy working on together. You can cut the pieces to size and allow your child to do the joining. Both of you can paint and stain. Sounds like a great way to spend a day!

Electrical Cord Covers

There are always functional items that get in the way of a beautifully designed room, and electrical cords are one of them. However, you can create easy fabric cord covers that will hide ugly cords and become a nice additional accent to the room.

Project note

To determine the amount of fabric needed for this project, consider that you will be making a tube of fabric twice the length of the cord or chain you are covering. The width of the fabric cut depends on the width of what you are covering, but a basic measurement is about 5 inches wide.

Steps

1 Measure the length of the cord you wish to cover.

For an electrical cord, consider making the cover 2 inches wide. (This allows for the plug to travel through the tube.) For a chain, make sure you add at least ½ inch to the width of the chain to allow for bunching and seam allowance.

2 Cut enough fabric to make the 2-inch tube twice the length of the cord. For width, cut the strips at 5 inches to accommodate a ½-inch seam allowance.

3 Pin and machine-stitch as many strips of fabric together as needed to cover the cord at double the length.

4 Fold the long strip in half lengthwise with right sides facing and pin along the long edge, keeping the ends open; machine-stitch in place.

5 Remove the pins and begin the process of turning the tube right side out by attaching the safety pin to one end, and then pushing the pin through the tube with your fingers until it comes out the other end. Grab the fabric and continue pulling until the tube is completely right side out. Remove the safety pin and iron the tube flat.

6 Fold the raw edges back into one end of the tube and insert the electrical cord into the tube, pushing the plug through to the other end. When the cover is completely on the cord, arrange and scrunch it to your liking, fold the other raw edge into the tube at the end and plug in the lamp. ∎

From Shari

This is a great decorating detail that allows you to add a chandelier where there is no electrical outlet in the ceiling. Just swag the chandelier over from a wall outlet, and cover the cord with a custom-made electrical cord cover. The cord cover makes the chandelier look like it was meant to be there, instead of added as an afterthought.

Accessory Pillows

Don't let your accessory pillows be a last-minute addition. Spend some time thinking about the detailing, the mixture of coordinating fabrics or the buttons, bows and tassels that can be added. Handmade pillows really can become works of art if you take your time and enjoy the entire process of making them.

Fabric or multiple fabrics of your choice

Matching sewing thread

Pillow form (if not covering an existing pillow)

Embellishments as desired

MATERIALS ON HAND

Fabric measuring tape

Cutting mat

Straightedge

Rotary cutters or scissors

Pins

Sewing machine

Iron and ironing board

Needle

Project note

This project is written for a simple accessory pillow slipcover. However, check the tip for ideas on creating more elaborate pillows.

Steps

1 Begin by measuring the width and height of the pillow to be covered. Double the width and add 5 inches for seams and overlap. For the height, add 1¼ inches for seam allowances. Cut a long rectangle to these dimensions.

2 Hem the short ends by folding the fabric over ½ inch twice and machine-stitching in place.

3 With the right side of the fabric facing up, fold the short ends to the center and overlap 3 inches. Check the width of the pillow cover to make sure it still is wide enough for the finished width of the pillow. Adjust the overlap accordingly.

4 Pin the top and bottom of the pillow cover, and machine-stitch in place. Clip the corners, trim the seam allowances, and turn the pillow cover right side out.

5 Iron the pillow cover flat, and insert your old pillow or new pillow form! ∎

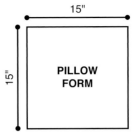

15"

15"

PILLOW FORM

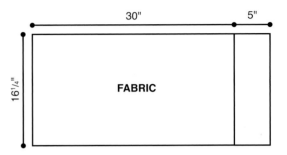

30"   5"

16¼"

FABRIC

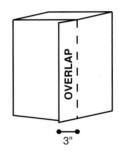

OVERLAP

3"

Overlap short ends of fabric

This same pillow slipcover can be made in three pieces instead of one so the front face can be embellished. For this, add 1¼ inches to the width and height of the pillow. Then, create a pillow front from several fabrics. Add trims, bows or buttons— whatever types of embellishments that please you. For the back, cut two pieces of fabric at one half the measurement of the width of the pillow plus 3⅛ inches for overlap, seams and hems. The height will be the height of the pillow plus 1¼ inches for seams.

TIP